A Witness

of Miracles

A Witness

of Miracles

Esperanza Rivera

To order additional copies of this book, contact:
Xlibris Corporation
1-888-795-4274
www.Xlibris.com
Orders@Xlibris.com
123837

Contents

Dedication

To Davey, my dearly beloved son, I dedicate this book to you in the hope that you will read it and know how much I love you and Christee. Since you were little, you would always say, "Don't hold me. Hold the baby." You were the big brother, but you were my baby too. Please know how much I appreciated all your love and care for Christee. All those times you defended her and allowed her to "get away with it." You were always her champion.

Son, I am sorry if, while immersed in my broken heart, I neglected to tell you I love you and I neglected to help you in dealing with your own sorrow and grieving. You too had a great loss, and you were right: you lost your sister and your best friend all in one day.

I also want to thank you for disagreeing with me and setting me straight when I wanted to run, hide from everyone, and sell the house. When I thought I could just shut those memories and be liberated of pain and sorrow. Thank you for your strength and foresight that I would change my mind and love every part of that house again as you and Christee were so much part of it and when you so passionately whispered to me, "All my memories of Christee are here in this house."

What is a miracle? Who am I, and what is my spiritual, theological, or educational background to even begin to discuss this subject?

Let's be clear that I am not proclaiming or asserting to be a saint, to be gifted, or to be a martyr to whom God has indeed intervened and presented a mission of miracles for the world to see and which then are documented for pursuit of religious sanctioning or otherwise.

No, not those miracles that the Bible is so full of, but the miracles that happen every day to someone like you and me, yet we are blind and oblivious to them and ignore the fact that the hand of God is in our lives constantly and take those events, happenings, and life itself for granted. And God goes without praise or an undemanding thank-you, and we go on and continue to be empty and unfulfilled, thinking God is not there and certainly not listening to our prayers.

This is not a religious book nor is it intended to proselytize, convert, or change anyone's opinion or religious belief.

This story is about a series of life events, normal and ordinary—or perhaps *not*. You can reflect on that!

Preface

I did not start out thinking of writing a book. Neither did I think that anyone would be interested in knowing Christee's life. I knew that friends and family knew her well and therefore knew her life. No need for a book

But it all started while I was at the cemetery, feeling sad, crying, and reliving the events of Christee's death.

I must admit I was very angry and could not move past the fact that she was so young, full of life, and did not deserve to die; she was only twenty-three years old! How could God allow this to happen?

AND after weeks of reliving the same scenes in my head, I realized that Christee's life was not just the events that led to her death; she didn't just exist for those few weeks. So I thought I needed to find something that would not necessarily ease my pain but look at Christee's life in its entirety, concentrate on her life, treasure every day of her life, and not grieve in anger and only see the last few weeks of her life.

I began to think and write about her birth, how happy I was, and as I kept writing, I came to realize that He could have taken her on that very first day of her life. Oh, my God, she was not breathing at the time she was born!

And as I reflected, I could only say, "Oh God, forgive me." How many parents lose their children at birth? And here I was complaining because I had her for twenty-three beautiful years.

This is my story, and you are welcome to journey with me in my memories, my beliefs, and into my family's life. You can question my beliefs and how I dealt with my life, but do not question the love for my family and veracity of the events that I describe and relate to you as it all happened and were witnessed by many members of my family and close friends, not just me.

Whether those who witness and recall the events as I do feel like I do or have reached the same conclusions and beliefs as I do, only they will tell you.

And if you happen to be one of those blessed souls that witness some of the events I mention here, I invite you to think and reflect on the graces our Lord has also bestowed upon you not because of my Christee but because of His love for you.

God is great! God has blessed me with so much. I don't mean money, as I have none, but with so many beautiful people around me who love me and support so many of my ideas and ventures throughout my life and, more importantly, who were there to help me and guide me while I was trying to raise my children, develop a career, and plan for a future full of happiness, success, and no heartbreak or sorrow.

So many beautiful memories I have, and I would love to share them all with you, but it would be hard to pick one from them all. However, God has granted some *miracles* in my life, and those I can and will attempt to relate and describe to you, for I feel I have an obligation to share with everyone the greatness of my Lord and how He intervened and presented Himself in my life and allowed me to witness the greatness of His works and miracles through my family and mainly through my children Davey and Christee.

What Is a Miracle?

Well, in my miniscule research I found the following:

Miracle: An extraordinary event attributed to a supernatural power. (*Britannica Concise Encyclopedia*)

Miracle:

1. An effect or extraordinary event in the physical world that surpasses all known human or natural powers and is ascribed to a supernatural cause.
2. Such an effect or event manifesting or considered as a work of *God*. (Dictionary.com)

A *miracle* is an unexpected event attributed to divine intervention. Sometimes an event is also attributed [in part] to a *miracle worker*, SAINT, or religious leader. A miracle is sometimes thought of as a perceptible interruption of the laws of nature. Others suggest that God may work *with* the laws of nature to perform what people perceive as miracles.

Theologians say that, with divine providence, God regularly works through created nature yet is free to work without, above, or against it as well. (*Wikipedia*)

A miracle is often considered a fortuitous event: compare with an ACT OF GOD. *Wikipedia*

In casual usage,"miracle" may also refer to any statistically unlikely but beneficial event, (such as surviving a natural disaster), or simply a "wonderful" occurrence, regardless likelihood, such as a birth. Other miracles might be:

survival of a terminal illness, escaping a life threatening situation or 'beating the odds.' Some coincidences are perceived to be miracles. Wikipedia

It is also documented that a belief in miracles exists in all cultures and nearly all religions.

So knowing the above definition and what the dictionaries and theologians say, would you recognize a miracle if you witness one or just take it for granted that "it is what it is."

Would you even know you were witnessing a miracle?

Would someone have to tell you or point out that YOU were the recipient of a miracle?

Would you even consider believing in such a thing?

Did you ever ask, pray, hope, or just express a request to God for a miracle and later found yourself questioning, "Where were you, God, when I needed you?" If so, then you must read my story.

Chapter 1

Blessings

I have thanked God many times for giving me wonderful parents, brothers and sisters, two beautiful children, and a wonderful husband—a friend and partner with whom I have shared most of my adult life and who has helped me through life's expected and unexpected trials and tribulations. Whose love has been unconditional and has been demonstrated time and time again, from the effortless hand-holding while taking a walk to the most awesome conversations about God and how He has a plan for each and every one of us and, through the most heart-wrenching pain, anguish, and sadness in our lives, a soft and tender embrace while we both cried. Thank you, David.

Is this luck or providence? Indeed, God's plan.

I have chosen to start this book not when Christee was born or when she got sick but on a very specific year to illustrate how my frame of mind was when I said I was a witness. How life happens, and sometimes, we just go along for the ride without enjoying it or savoring every step of the way and stopping to smell every rose or take in every smile! It has always been very hard for me to SMILE.

Chapter 2

What Did Just Happen?

In 1992, after ten years of a blissful and happy marriage, successful careers, and two beautiful children, we found ourselves going through a crisis and were in need of making difficult decisions. THAT is when I experienced what I called then a "sighting" as I had no clue what it was at that time, so I named it as such.

I was driving at night and on my way home to my children and husband. My heart was in pain, and I was full of worries and apprehensions for my children, me, and yes, my husband whom I adored, but I thought that a decision needed to be made that night. There were problems!

The drive I had made every day for many years now seemed lonely and strange. The route I had taken for years suddenly looked strange.

I came to a stoplight, and while I was waiting for the light to turn and proceed on my way to make a life-changing decision, deep in thought, praying and hoping to find the words to speak to my husband, all of a sudden I saw something at that stop that I had never seen before.

Well, I had seen the marquee before that displays the name and sign of a church. I had seen that sign many times over the years, but never had I seen it as I saw it that night.

I was staring ahead and waiting for the traffic light to turn when an intense and dazzling bright light hit my face, and as I stared at it more, I began to see a white dove. The dove was on the marquee all by itself. I could almost see it in motion, flying toward me. It was a big white dove and emanated a warm light, or so I felt. I was almost in a daze, and there was such calm effect in me.

I felt the warmth of a bright light, like when someone gives you a big embrace and holds you there for a moment or two, and it felt good—oh God, it felt so good. I forgot that I was sitting right there in my car. I don't know how long I sat there, staring at the dove and feeling the warmth with such an inner peace, almost like an embrace.

A sound from a car horn and an angry motorist brought me back to awareness. The white dove looked at me and then the light was off, and the moment was gone.

The light had changed again, and I was still there. The marquee remained, showing the name of the church, but there was no bright light or white dove anywhere.

I still go by there, and by instinct, I slow down to get the red light for me to sit there and watch the marquee, hoping that I can see and feel the warmth and bright light and the white dove that I saw that night.

I have not seen the dove again—not yet anyways.

It was then that I began to think about *God's miracles* and *angels* and wondered if we all had *our assigned guardian angels* and how many miracles one was allowed to have.

Chapter 3

A Holiday!

Life was good again, and I was enjoying every minute of it!

Memorial weekend ahead, in 1994, a carne asada was planned at my house. I just loved all the holidays and long weekends as they meant family time at my house. Swimming, eating, bonding, and making plans for our future and those of our children.

A phone call came in from my sister, Rosa, telling me that Mom had been rushed to the hospital.

I remember telling my husband, "Take care of the kids. I'll be right back. I'll have to go and see what is wrong with Mom. Later on I called him and said, "Cancel all plans. Mom is dying."

The diagnosis and prognosis of a brain aneurism were not good. The doctors said, "Five percent she might live, but most likely, no vision, hearing, or movement, or she might not be able to speak or remember anything or recognize anyone."

Did the doctor say she might live?

All her children and Dad were there and were all visibly worried and upset. My thoughts went back to a few years earlier when, on a Memorial weekend, we had received a similar call announcing *Nina* Lupe (our maternal grandmother) had died. So I feared the worse and reflected, *What a Memorial weekend indeed.*

It is in this environment of despair and anguish that one remembers to pray and pray hard and ask God for his mercy and proceed to make promises and request for a miracle.

My sisters and I did not leave the hospital, day and night, and we were there, praying and praying. My mom always prayed the Rosary and had taught us to pray, but I don't remember, ever, when all of us prayed together with such fervor and passion.

At times we cried and then we would laugh; nerves, anxiety, and fear of losing Mom. Mom was the *matriarch* of the family; nothing happened without Mom's input, approval, or just talking it over with her. What would we do without her? No, none of us even wanted to think about that. Instead we laughed at how just before Mom lost consciousness; she began to tell each of us what to do.

She always told us that she loved each and every one of us in a very, very special way but all the same. That she knew each of her eight children very well and what each one was like, the responsibilities we were willing to take, and the strengths we each had.

You see, on that day, she told me, *"Go back to work. No need for you to be here. You don't like to waste time and don't have any patience to sit around. Go back to work, and figure out what needs to be done."*

All I wanted was to be there, close to her and close to my sisters and brother, and I stayed, but it was so true what she said.

Mom, Margarita, was an only child and urged us, her children, once we were married, to have children, not as many as she had but at least two. *"So they won't be lonely, and you will be able to provide for them and have time to dedicate to each of them."*

Mom and Dad, Ramon de la Cruz, had worked so hard for us to have a good life: a roof over our heads, food, and love. She never went on a vacation or even went to the movies because all she ever did was work and work for her children. Unselfish, loving, and caring, and now, she was dying or, as the doctors said, "might live" but without memory or movement.

What happened to fairness and justice?

Where was God? My mother was a good mother and a good person. Shouldn't He have mercy on her?

Would God grant me, my family, and my mother a miracle? Will she live without any brain damage or physical incapacity?

We all prayed.

Chapter 4

Happy and Healthy

When your loved ones are healthy and happy and all seems to be going right, you pray and you go to church and you believe in whatever it is you believe in because ALL is well, and there are no worries.

I remember sitting down to talk to my husband and the children and asking their opinion about me going back to school and telling them that it would have to be a family decision as the family would have many sacrifices because of it, such as money issues and chores around the house would have to be managed differently as I would have to do lots of homework and studying.

What awesome children God gave me! They did not hesitate, and they each adopted some of my chores aside from the ones they already had.

So we were happy, the children were healthy, both my husband and I had jobs, and I was in law school, something I had put off to get married and have a family.

I believed God was a loving father, and as a loving father, He was expected to be there when you needed him with a loving heart and open arms. No need to make any other efforts. You knew you loved Him, and He loved you, so He was expected to take care of you and your loved one, right?

Is that what happened? Did I take God for granted? Was I not praising him as I should have?

Maybe when we are so happy and all is going well, we let our guard down, not intentionally, but complacently, we forget to thank God for our blessing and continue to ask for His mercy.

All I know is that I found myself again in that desperate mode of seeking God and feeling like he was not there, a sense of abandonment, so again, I found myself praying and praying hard not for me, my children, or husband but for my dear friend Raul.

Chapter 5

An Invitation

In May 1996, my brother-in-law Raul R. Perez, husband to my sister Rosi and who had introduced me to my husband, called me and invited me to get together with my sister Rosi for shopping while he was submitting himself to gallbladder surgery. Only Raul would think about us going shopping instead of being there at the hospital, waiting for him.

He was a very likeable guy, and I held him in very high esteem, although we joked at times that he must not like me much since he had introduced me to David, which resulted in a marriage, so we joked and teased about it and became very good friends.

I declined the invitation to go shopping; studying and homework were my excuse. After that, he would not hear of me going and sitting in the waiting room. Although I said I could study while waiting, he said no, and I stayed home.

On that May day, Raul was diagnosed with fourth-stage gallbladder cancer, and I was not there for him or my sister. I thanked God that I did have time to apologize to him. He laughed and said, "It's okay. You didn't want to go shopping anyway." And that was that.

I couldn't understand how God could do something like this to someone so nice, young, and full of life and energy to help others in their personal or business lives.

How can this be happening, God?

Raul, a friend to many, a loving husband to a young wife, and father of two young children who needed him. A community leader, who had fought against the odds and persevered in his goals in the city of Huntington Park and, after six consecutive elections, had victoriously come to be the first Latino mayor of that city, a rising Latino political figure in California. Yes, my dear friend whom I admired so much and certainly deserving of God's mercy was dying.

What happened to fairness and justice?

Where was God again? Had He answered that for me yet?

And I prayed, *Jesus, here I am again, asking and praying for a miracle, making promises to be a better person, a better Christian, and a good-service Catholic.*

Jesus, please save Raul, my good friend, my compadre (Davey's godfather), my brother-in-law. Those were my prayers over and over.

And I questioned God and my faith. *Would God hear me and grant me a miracle?*

How many miracles per family, or per person, would God grant?

Is there a magic number of prayers, requests, and promises that one must make before He listens?

Had I not thanked Him?

Did I not praise his name well enough?

I was angry, yet I wanted him to hear my sister, his children, the family, and me—yes, again—me asking Him for mercy and a miracle.

We all prayed like before, with humility, with passion, and with all our love and waited and waited for that miracle.

Because of those prayers, requests, and promises I made on that day, I later called my church and became a service Catholic in the religious education ministry where I continue to serve and where I find so much peace, love, and joy. Where so many families constantly touch my life and where I have learned so much of my faith.

Chapter 6

Labor Day Weekend

September 4, 2006

Internally I have dreaded holidays and long weekends to the point that I almost fear them. I love the "family get-togethers," as I called them. Being together, sharing with family, seeing the children grow, catching up with what is going on and who is doing what and where are they going to college and all. But trepidation, apprehension, and anxiety have always been present in my heart and mind since Nina Lupe died on a Memorial weekend back in 1987.

Today, that anxiety, fear, and worry were more present than ever. Christee was sick, very sick, and in the hospital on a holiday, on a long weekend.

Oh, God, had I learned to pray yet?

Was my faith strong enough for whatever was to happen?

Where did I fail you, God?

Where are you? Are you listening to me? Have I tired you?

God, please grant me a miracle? Please, just this one?

And I prayed.

Chapter 7

Twenty-Three Years Before . . .

On August 21, 1983, we were celebrating David Lee Jr.'s first birthday party. We had such a wonderful celebration at Salt Lake Park, in the city of Huntington Park, where we lived.

Davey's actual birthday is August 25, but we had decided to celebrate early as I was pregnant and ready to give birth to our second child.

Caesarian procedure. The doctor said I could choose the date from the twenty-fifth to the twenty-ninth of the month for the baby to be born. I can still remember how excited I was. I could celebrate their birthdays together, and they would be very good to each other, best friends, having the same birthday. Growing together, finding out about life close to each other.

I always wanted twins, and this was going to be the closest I would get to having twins. The children would be sharing their birthday—well, the day and month, NOT the year obviously, but one year apart.

The baby's "birth" was scheduled for August 25. We still did not know if the baby was a boy or a girl, but her name would be *Christee Lee* if she was a girl!

David and I had decided on the name Christee Lee while dating and making plans for our "happily ever after" days!

I came up with the name *Christee Lee* one day at the Florence Methodist Church where David sang and directed the choir. One of the ladies there was going through a book of baby names and showed it to me.

I looked up the name "*Christy* = follower of Christ; *Christie*, beautiful Christian." I just loved the name. But I also liked David's middle name, Lee, so I came up with the name CHRISTEE, double *e* to be different and go with *Lee* as a middle name. I loved it then, and I love it now.

My precious Christee was a follower of Jesus and a beautiful Christian.

Life was good, and we were happy, and we prayed that the baby would be healthy. Boy or girl, we didn't care; we just had to figure out a boy's name if it happened to be a boy.

Did I tell you that the C-section was scheduled for August 25?

I remember, in the middle of the night of August 21, the labor pains began, but I didn't want to tell David anything. After all, it wasn't time yet; the birth had been scheduled for August 25, so it was not time yet.

I lay down and walked around, huffing and puffing, thinking I was just tired from all the running around with Davey's birthday party.

At around 3:00 a.m. on August 22, the water bag broke, and there was no denying any longer; I was having a baby!

I remember waking David up and telling him what was going on. He got up, called his parents, and asked if they could come to the house to stay with Davey and then went into the walk-in closet.

I was ready, waiting in the front room, and then I realized that there was no David in sight and went to the bedroom and saw David still in the closet, just standing there. I said, "David, we have to go NOW." He just responded, "I don't know what to wear."

When David's parents got home, he finally was ready, and we rushed to the hospital. That baby wasn't waiting for the twenty-fifth, or for anyone's "schedule."

On the way to the hospital, David pulled into the supermarket's parking lot, and I looked at him, questioning, "Why are we stopping?"

He simply said, "I used all the camera film during Davey's party," and got out of the car.

I was screaming with labor pains when he came back with the film. I think, at that point, he finally realized that it was happening, and he drove, or flew, to the hospital.

He later apologized and explained that he didn't want to not have pictures for the second child as most people did. At first, I was furious, being in such pain and all, but after the baby was born and seeing the pictures, all was okay. We got the most beautiful pictures of our precious little girl that day.

Chapter 8

Sit Tight and Wait

At the hospital, we were told that there were "other births ahead of you," to sit tight, and wait.

Can anyone just "wait" or "hold off" the birth of a child?

I remember they put me in a gurney and rolled me into a room. I was so scared the nurse came in and said the doctor was in with another patient.

The pains intensified, and the doctor was not available, yet the nurse spoke to David and then an injection was administered, and I was very upset because no one asked me if I wanted it or even told me what it was for.

I was angry with David for allowing it and with the nurse for sneaking behind me and just sticking me with it. I am sure I was harsh with both. The nurse said after the fact that "the doctor ordered it." I argued, but it was too late; it was done. "It will calm you down while you wait for the doctor."

Finally, the doctor came and surgery began.

As John Lennon said, *"Life is what happens while you are busy making other plans,"* and Christee Lee was born on August 22, 1983 at 7:19 a.m., without waiting for the very carefully "scheduled date" or the fact that I wanted them to "have the same birthday" or for my "closest to twins I'll ever get" wish.

I was awake during the surgery and felt the pulling and tugging of the C-section procedure. I remember the doctor talking to David and the others in the room. I remember when he said, "It's a girl," BUT I did not hear Christee cry.

I felt a final pull and knew she was out of my womb. I was very excited. David held my hand all throughout, and I could see his face and his nervous smile had turned into a tense and worried face.

They did not let me hold the baby. I don't remember if David held the baby. I could hear commotion going on although I could not understand what they were saying. Their words were no longer words of joyfulness but more of urgency, matter of fact.

All of a sudden, it was just David and I in the room. I remember I kept asking David, who had been there beside me and had seen Christee being born, "What is going on?" He kept saying, "She is okay. They are cleaning her up, and they'll bring her in a minute."

I knew something was wrong, I had heard my son's cry after he was born, a C-section too. I knew what to expect, yet this time, it was different. I knew something was going on, and no one was telling me.

A mother's heart knows but sometimes does not want to accept what is happening. It pretends to ignore, so I waited.

Chapter 9

Tiny Little Hands

She was a bit purple still when they finally brought my baby to me. I saw her and held my baby girl, my Christee Lee, but only for a few seconds because they said she needed to be in an incubator.

I remember asking the nurse, "Why an incubator? She was a full-term baby." The nurse just said, "Doctor's orders."

She was little and fragile. She weighed only five pounds and fourteen ounces; she was twenty-two inches long. My Davey had been seven pounds and nineteen inches long. She didn't seem that small to me, but they took her back to the incubator and kept her there until the next day when I went to see her.

Christee was a beautiful baby, and I fell in love with her right away. I was amazed and mesmerized with her tiny little hands, with her long and slender fingers, her fully shaped fingernails, and the most beautiful warm rosy color on them. Her hands, their texture and color, would later reveal and manifest something else.

I later learned that Christee was not breathing when she was pulled out of the womb. She had been rushed to be given oxygen; she was placed in the incubator to monitor her and ensure she was fine. *She was fine now, right?*

I remember David telling me how scared he was when he first saw her; she was not breathing. My poor husband, he had to endure that by himself although, of course, I was there. He had carried that burden of knowing she was not breathing, yet he kept telling me, "She is going to be all right."

I do remember thanking God that she was okay and "complete" after I had counted her toes and fingers. I also thanked God that I was fine too. I could see my children grow old.

But did I understand then what really had happened?

A few days later, on the way home from the hospital, we stopped at St. Matthias Church in Huntington Park where Dave and I got married, and I presented Christee to God, and Father Gorman, our priest and friend, gave Christee a blessing. What a beautiful moment!

Christee went from the hospital to the church to meet her Savior.

Lord, keep her safe and healthy, I prayed. As I had prayed when Davey was born and we had brought him to church too, right after the hospital.

Chapter 10

411 or Was It 911?

Parenting and infant/children's CPR classes. Before I had the children, I was determined to be prepared and ready for whatever foreseeable or unforeseeable needs presented with the children.

I was on top of the world: a loving and caring husband, two beautiful and healthy children, and we were both employed. I was going to be the best working mom ever!

I remember being pregnant with my second child and with my toddler on hand every weekend at every open house like Lookie Lous, until we found the perfect house for us to share as a family.

On January 1984 we moved to La Mirada, Davey was just one year and five months Christee was five months.

I remember thanking God that we had a home, where our children would be able to grow with love and be safe.

Christee was just under six months when she developed a cold, stuffy nose, and mild fever; David said to put Vicks on her feet and on her chest, and I did. I learned, since then, that is the worse thing you can do, but I did not know any better then. The parenting classes had not addressed that particular subject!

Christee got so hot her cheeks were red; they almost looked like they were glowing. Then she began to convulse and then pass out; she was not breathing! I panicked and began to yell and called 411 who told me to hang up and call 911. Meanwhile, David, who had heard the yelling, came and took her from me and unbundled her. Yes, I had wrapped her in a blanket. She was sick, right?

I managed to call 911, and meanwhile, David gave the baby, Christee, CPR. By the time the paramedics and fire department showed up, Christee was breathing and conscious again. They were very nice and told us NEVER to put Vicks on an infant with fever, never to wrap a baby in a bundle when they have fever, and to follow up with her doctor. They were so nice, and yes, they made me feel so stupid. What happened to the parenting classes? The first real test, and I had failed my Christee.

I now realize how blessed Christee was. God kept a constant watch over her.

Our life was happy and uneventful for a few months.

Chapter 11

Her Little Bruised Face

Christee was almost one year old. She was healthy, and like all children, she was happy.

Unlike Davey, that had started to walk at eight months and actually spoke, more than Mom and Dad, at ten months, Christee was developing much slower. She was quiet and calm but very curious. You would see her crawling or running with the use of her walker. She could get in trouble even though she did not walk yet.

On her first birthday party, Christee was not walking and still had no teeth, but we were ready to celebrate her birthday in a big way!

The celebration, along with all the family and closest friends, was going to be a big one. We were celebrating both birthdays, Davey's and Christee's, on August 25, 1984. I still wanted to celebrate both birthdays together and hoped that they would not mind as they grew older.

The night before the birthday party, some family and friends came over to assist with the preparations, food, and decorations. Christee was sitting in her walker, moving all over the den. Everyone was busy and doing something; I was in the kitchen.

All of a sudden, I heard Christee's walker closer, and as I turned around, I saw the walker fastly moving toward the edge of the step from the kitchen to the den—it was one step down and about a foot high—and it was too late.

She pushed off, and the walker rolled to the edge, and I just saw it move smoothly, gliding and tipping over the edge of the step. The walker landed on its side, and Christee came off it. Her face was on the floor—a hard cement floor with linoleum—and she screamed.

Oh dear God, I couldn't stop her fall!

I should have paid more attention to Christee instead of all the party preparation, but the fact is that I did not, and she fell and hurt herself. She was crying and visibly in pain.

Why does it always happen that way? Why can't we foresee some of the things that children do, or was that just me?

We rushed her to the hospital. She was crying, and I just knew she had a broken nose and my heart ached. I should have been carrying her, taking care of her, and not keeping her in that awful walker. How did she get to the kitchen, which was one step up? It really didn't matter how. The fact was I was the mom and should have protected her.

I was mortified having to explain to the nurses and doctor what had happened. I felt their eyes looking at me with such disdain, blaming me and thinking, *What a careless mother.* Well, anyways, that is exactly how I felt—guilty.

The doctor performed a brief exam and sent her for x-rays and then we just waited and waited for the results. Christee had calmed down and now wanted to sleep, but I was terrified of her falling asleep. Someone said that "It's not good for babies to sleep after a blow to their head." I don't even know who said that, but I was terrified. How could I have been so careless with my baby? And now instead of allowing her to rest, there I was trying to bounce her up and keep her awake.

After the doctor reviewed the x-rays, he said, "You are lucky she didn't break her neck. She does not have a broken nose either. She'll be in pain for a couple of days and will have a black and blue face too but should be okay in a few days."

I am not making any excuse now, but in retrospect, there had been plenty of adults there helping out, yet Christee still managed to get in trouble. Was that a sign of things to come?

The next day, she had a bruised face and a beautiful smile, and that was her first birthday party.

My children were one and two years old. What a wonderful time, and I promised to be more careful with my children.

Chapter 12

Electrifying Personality

Christee could walk now, and she was curious about everything. Of course, I got covers for all the electrical sockets—boy, was I good or what? I told you I took parenting classes, didn't I?

I came home one day after work, and I found the babysitter was a bit quiet. I always came home and played with the kids, and Socorro, or Co, as Davey called her, would sit and watch her *novelas*. But on that day, she did not want to let go of Christee and kept telling me to "Rest or play with Davey. I'll hold Christee. She is not feeling well." Of course, I heard that, and it was enough for me to go and take her away.

Co was a very nice lady and took good care of my kids, but at times, she was way overprotective of the children, and if they got a scratch or bruise when she was off, she would get very upset with me. I always appreciated everyone that helped me with the children, but at times, she was overwhelming and almost as if she was their mother and not me.

Calmly and with a smile, I took Christee from her and then asked, "What happened to Christee today? What did she get into?"

And that's all it took; Co began to cry, and Davey began the story.

"Christee was crawling around the den, trying to pull the covers of the electrical sockets, but she couldn't, then Christee got the clock." And Davey showed me the clock. It was a wedding gift we had received. It was a miniature plastic replica of a grandfather clock, and the pendulum was a plastic doll, a little girl swinging. When I looked at the little doll,

I could see that it had been partially melted and was only hanging from one wire and not the two that it used to have.

I was holding Christee, and I could see that she was fine, but Co then took the mitten off her right hand, and I saw the burn on her hand, and Davey showed me the wall socket. Christee just showed me her hand, and she smiled.

Co had applied medicine, and although it did not look bad, it looked painful, and I took her to the After Hours Medical Care. We paid so much for medical insurance for the children, but it was money well spent, especially for and with Christee. It turned out to be, thank God, only a first-degree burn; they gave her some ointment and baby Tylenol, and she was fine.

After that day, I think Co respected my parenting skills more as that incident had happened on her watch and understood that Christee was quick and curious, and she was bound to get into trouble many more times.

Chapter 13

Almost Drowned

A house with a swimming pool means danger and responsibilities in safeguarding and minimizing those dangers; we were aware of them. I was not a good swimmer, and being fast to panic, it was decided that unless David was in the swimming pool watching the children, I would not take them to the pool area by myself specially since Davey was a handful—or was it Christee?

It was also decided that when company was over, the rule called that the parent of a child entering the pool would be there, watching their child unless another adult volunteer to take care of that child. Since it was all family, we felt comfortable telling them the rules and enforcing them too. We wanted a fun and safe environment for our children and theirs too. It happens that when there are too many adults, no one watches the children.

The rules called for no running, no diving, and oh yes, that the undivided attention of an adult was required at all times while a child was in the pool area; otherwise, the gate would be locked.

It was an early Saturday morning in summer, and David took the children out to the swimming pool to clean around and prepare the barbecue; company would soon come over. We had family over almost every weekend during the summer. They all loved to come over to the pool, and we enjoyed having them over.

I was in the house, cleaning and preparing whatever it was that I was going to serve for lunch when I heard David yelling at Davey and Christee crying. As I rushed to the backdoor, I saw David coming in with Christee in his arms. She was soaking wet, and David looked angry. Davey was crying, and David turned to me and said, "Don't ask."

David wouldn't let go of Christee, so I went to get a towel to dry her, and when I came back, I heard David tell the children, "You two won't be allowed in the pool area for the next ten years even if I am there!"

The kids began to cry again, and I asked, "What happened? Did Davey wet Christee?" Poor Davey. He was mischievous and therefore often got blamed for something he had not done or even thought of doing—well, not yet.

There was silence from David. Then Davey, the three-year-old began, "Mommy, Mommy, Christee was running, and she fell in the swimming pool together with Federico." Federico was Christee's patch doll; she carried him all the time. "And I pulled her out." I was in shock, and Davey continued, "I was behind her telling her not to run, but she did anyway, and when she fell in, I bent down and pull her hair and then Papi [as the children called their father] was there."

I didn't hear the rest of what he was saying. Panic set in, and all I could do was look at David; he was still holding Christee, and now I understood why he was holding her so tightly and yet so tenderly.

David's face, which had shown anger before, softened, and he turned to Davey and said, "I am sorry. I didn't know what had happened!" And he hugged him and held both children there for a long, long time.

Davey always did display such common sense, even at that age, and was always vigilant about children getting into trouble. Apparently, Christee fell into the swimming pool while running, and Davey, her Big Brother, as she later referred to him, pulled her out of the swimming pool by her hair. Christee cried, David turned around and saw that, and he assumed the rest.

Because David was so scared of what could have happened, he just issued punishment, or should I say outrageous punishment, without having found out what had really happened. "You two won't be allowed in the pool area for the next ten years even if I am there!"

Swimming classes began and continued until those kids were good at it. They even took a course at Biola University where they were taught how to survive in the water for hours with nothing but their own clothes.

I don't think we were negligent parents. David had been there, taking care of them and playing with them. It was just in a blink of an eye that David looked the other way, and she fell in. That was Christee for you: quiet, unpredictable, yet very charismatic.

The usual back and forth as to who was doing what and who was taking care of Christee, and it was soon discovered that if Christee was around, not much work was going to be done. She needed and wanted all the attention, and we had to watch her as there was always the risk of her getting into trouble. And boy, was she good at it!

Davey was always near his sister and knew that she could get in trouble real easy. He got her out of trouble or stopped her from getting into trouble so many times. Like I said before, he has always had very good critical-thinking head on, plus I think he knew he would be blamed for whatever happened. He did not just keep her safe but other children too, like Francine, a little girl my mother-in-law took care of, and some of the younger cousins.

But there were so many other times when he just couldn't keep her out of trouble and not for lack of trying. He was such a good brother to her. She loved him so much and always looked up to him and, many times, said, "How come I am not like Davey that thinks about things first . . . I just do and then they are wrong or bad."

Davey & Christee
Superman & Wonder Woman

Chapter 14

Cystic Fibrosis

Christee was about eighteen months when we began to notice she had clammy hands, complained of pain in her hands, and didn't want to eat.

It was both her hands; otherwise, I would have thought of the electrical socket incident. No, this was not the prior burn.

I took her to the doctor, and they did the normal and routine exams and said it was normal that they play more rather than eat and not to worry. But she would not eat, and I insisted that it required more than just routine exams.

So after a couple of months of different exams and medicines, the doctor began to notice other symptoms, and he sent us to Long Beach Memorial hospital with a long list of lab orders. We had never heard of some of the test names. I remember it was so overwhelming, and she was so little and crying, and my heart ached so much I just went through the motions but did not understand much of what was happening.

When I asked the doctor what that was all about, he declared that all the symptoms present were of cystic fibrosis and that he needed the labs immediately. I said okay, and I left his office in a daze. Cystic fibrosis—I had never heard of that illness before.

I remember going straight to the hospital with Christee. No cell phone then, and no time to waste, so I did not call David to tell him what was going on. At the hospital, they were all very nice to us. Christee was such a cute baby that everyone loved the faces she made. She did not complain much, and all the testing was done.

The technician told me they would send all the results to Dr. Muney, Christee's doctor, and not to worry about anything. He had such a big smile that I felt comforted and assured that all was well, and my baby was fine. I hugged my baby and went home.

I got home, put the baby to sleep, and called David. I told him what had happened at the doctors and that I had taken Christee to have all the lab work the doctor ordered. He kept asking what was it that Dr. Muney thought she had. I couldn't remember the name, and I told him something with *fibrosis*. I remember him saying, "Not cystic fibrosis." I said, "Yes, that's it," and then there was silence.

Did David know what a horrible disease that was?

I was so naive, ignorant, and unprepared. The dictionary. Where is the dictionary? I had so many dictionaries around the house, yet I couldn't find one soon enough. The dictionary read as follows:

> **Cystic fibrosis**, *a hereditary disease of the exocrine glands characterized by the production of thickened mucus that chronically clogs the bronchi and pancreatic ducts, leading to breathing difficulties, infection, and fibrosis.*

> **Fibrosis:** *The development in an organ of excess fibrous connective tissue.*

> **Fibrous**: *Containing, consisting of or resembling fibers.*

I don't think I understood much, but it did not sound good at all, and I didn't like the doctor's face when he told me to take her to the lab nor David's response once I told him what it was. I needed a medical dictionary.

When David got home, I was exhausted; he didn't want to talk much. I remember him telling me, "Let's just wait for the result," and he just played with the kids.

Not much I could do for today. I knew there was a medical dictionary at work, and I would find out the next day.

Chapter 15

A Diagnosis

I went to work the next day and went straight to the medical dictionary.

> **Cystic fibrosis** *is an inherited disease that causes thick, sticky mucus to build up in the lungs and digestive tract. It is one of the most common chronic lung diseases in children and young adults, and may result in early death, teens or early twenties.*

I was stunned; I couldn't believe what I was reading. One of the attorneys came in to ask how Christee was doing since he knew I had taken her to the doctor the day before.

I showed him the dictionary and told him that her doctor thought she had cystic fibrosis. He tried to comfort me. I don't remember if I was crying or not. I always tried to be so professional and keep personal life out of the workplace, but I do remember him being very concerned and telling me that I should ask for a second opinion once the results came back.

I went home early to be with the kids. When David got home, I told him I had looked up the illness again but this time in the medical dictionary. He hugged me, and we cried and prayed, prayed for our little girl. Yes, once again I prayed for a miracle that the results were all negative and that she did not have cystic fibrosis.

I learned early on that my mom had too many worries on her head and heart: there were eight children to worry about, and now, we all had our children that she worried about, so I didn't want her to know about Christee, not just yet.

I often prayed and thanked God that He did indeed spare my mother of some of my trials and tribulations, but I also missed having her near me, holding me, consoling me the way only a mother can do.

My mom was funny. She would often tell me that she had hardly slept, and when I would ask why, she would say, "I was trying to fix [she would give me a name of one of her children] his or her problems." She spent many sleepless nights trying to solve our problems; there were eight of us.

But she was a great mom; she never interfered or meddled in our marriages or even contradicted us as to our disciplinary actions when the children were present. She was awesome, gave us good advice when we asked for it, and not gratuitous.

But I had resolved that she would only hear of my problems, troubles, and tribulations within my marriage and my children only after said trials and tribulations were fixed or had no hope of being fixed. I loved her too much and saw her suffer so much that I did not want to contribute to it, having just said that.

I had to find a way to ask about our family's history regarding illness and specially lung diseases.

After conversations and sidestepping the actual questions, I learned that no one in our family had such disease. I didn't know anyone who had that, and we still had not heard from the doctor.

Lord, we cried and cried. The thought of Christee having an incurable *lung* disease was beyond comprehension; she was only a baby.

Chapter 16

I Believe in Prayer

After a few weeks of praying, crying, and no sleep, the doctor's appointment was arranged for us to go and find out the results.

David and I had worked out a system; since we both worked, when the children got sick, we took turns taking them to the doctor to avoid either of us missing much work and jeopardizing our employment. We had children, and we had a mortgage. Work ethic was ingrained in me; I saw my parents work and work even when they were sick.

But on that day, we both went to the doctor. On that day, we needed each other, and our baby needed us both there.

Christee and Davey had been very healthy children. Aside from Christee having allergies to almost every baby formula, she was healthy, and I was sure there was a mistake. I kept praying and asking God to please spare her and heal her of whatever it was that was making her sick. Somehow, I could not conceive of such illness for a child, and I prayed for all the children who may have had that disease. I was so scared.

Dr. Muney, I still remember his name. He was the first doctor I had ever seen taking his time to examine the children. He often let Davey hold the stethoscope to listen to his own heart, and once, he let Davey look into Christee's ear with the ear scope (Otoscope). I really liked him, but on that day, I was not sure I wanted to see him.

We did not wait much in the waiting room. He greeted us with a big smile and said that the testing was negative. Oh God, what a relief. I was holding Christee, and I hugged her, and I cried. "Thank you, Lord. Thank you, Lord." That's all I could say.

"We still don't know why she isn't eating, has clammy hands, mucus, and at times, is short of breath," Dr. Muney continued, "but the x-ray shows her lungs are clear and are clean." She had all the signs of cystic fibrosis, but all the tests were negative.

That was good news. Different medicines were prescribed to treat her although no diagnosis was given, and I was okay with that.

David and I, by then, had read so much about cystic fibrosis that we agreed to become members and donors to the Cystic Fibrosis Foundation, and we contributed each year and prayed for all those children that have such a horrible disease and prayed for all those parents too who have to endure seeing their children suffer so much.

Yes, God was there alongside Christee again.

Chapter 17

Two Religions, One God

We prayed; we went to church, both Catholic and Methodist. Dave and I had been married in both religions!

It wasn't that we thought we needed double insurance that the marriage would work by marrying in both religions; it was my mother and her sleepless nights.

At first, she was adamant that I had to be married in the Catholic church, but then I guess when she thought it over, she was concerned that David would not take the marriage seriously as he was not a Catholic, so she said it would probably be best to marry by his religion, and that way, she would know he would take the marriage seriously. I told you she was funny and reflected on everything to do with her children and solved their problems or "prospective" problems.

David and I decided to speak to my priest, Father Gorman of St. Mathias Church, and his minister, Rene. After all, they were friends; we often run into them in the community events.

They were both happy to celebrate our vows together at the Catholic church in both religions and in a bilingual ceremony. My mother was very happy: we were both going to take the marriage seriously.

Therefore, the children had been baptized in both religions. The priest and minister agreed the children would grow and choose their religion. We had agreed to participate in both churches. Both children were doing well, and Christee was still taking medications but was well overall and had stopped complaining about her hands. She could run and speak and went from being skinny to chubby and then skinny again.

Christee was almost three years old. She loved to be with her daddy and enjoyed to sing along with him. He was teaching her to sing. "Golden Slumbers" by the Beatles was the first song that Christee sang. David always used to sing it for her before she went to sleep, and she learned it and loved to sing it.

What wonderful memories I have, and I thank God for them, and I pray to God that my memory will serve me well for the rest of my days to praise him and reflect on all the joy and happiness there has been in my life. I guess the painful memories too.

Lord, help me. I do not want to dwell on the painful past.

Chapter 18

Car Wreck!

On Saturday morning, off to work I went, half days on Saturday. David was home and in charge of the children.

Davey was usually playing on his own, building some type of contraption or disassembling something to see what was inside. But he still kept an eye on Christee even if Daddy was there. Davey was such a grown-up. I remember there were so many times when I wanted to hold him; after all he was only one year older than Christee, but he would always say, "No, hold the baby, not me. I am big." He was so much taller and huskier than Christee. She was very petite and a lot shorter than Davey was that he did indeed look at lot older, but he was still my little boy.

I came back home in the early afternoon to find out that they had had a busy morning, and it went like this:

David went to the garage to tinker with the lawn mower, and the children had followed. Christee had asked if she could get in the car. David told them it was okay and saw them get in the car. My husband was and is a great father, but he could never tell the children NO.

The car was a 1952 Buick that was parked in the middle of the garage and an old collectible that David had bought for Davey, as if Davey needed a car—he was only four years old!

Do you know what a 1952 Buick car looks like or weighs? It is big and solid, pure metal. *When I went into the garage, I used to say it scared me with its big teeth in the front.*

David would later tell me that he had indeed told them, "Specifically not to touch anything." I don't know what my husband was thinking because we all know that telling someone, not just kids, not to touch something is like inviting them to touch it. Christee was no different than anyone else. As a matter of fact, she would, later in life, complain that she didn't understand why, at times, she would do things even against her better judgment.

Did I mention she was curious? After a while, she was no longer curious but daring.

And so the kids were in the car.

The neighbor, to the east side of the house, Jordie, was an eccentric Scottish man who became Dave's buddy; he told us no one in the neighborhood liked him. He was very nice to us and the children. Well, he called David over to the fence to ask him a question, and David walked out of the garage and to the fence.

I often told David, "Keep Christee next to you. Carry her. She weighs nothing and will save you the running around after her." She, in a blink of an eye, would find something to challenge us with.

And so while David was speaking to Jordie, Christee pulled the gear level off from park to reverse, and there the car went, down the driveway and across the street. The car came to a halting stop by crashing into a classic 1966 Mustang. I often thought this would make a good movie scene but not then and not with my children.

Yes, David saw, with dismay, the car just pass by, and Davey relayed later that he got out of the car to walk to the fence with Daddy, and when he saw the car moving, he "had tried to stop the car," but he couldn't stop it, so he moved out of the way. "And the car just kept rolling down the driveway, Mommy."

Can you imagine my poor little boy trying to stop the car for his little sister not to get in trouble? Yet had enough common sense to realize he could not stop the car and moved away. Thank you, Davey!

Dear God, I know you were there. My children were both alive.

As usual, David had issued punishment and Christee was admonished that she would not drive until she was forty years old and would have to repay him for the damage to the cars, the Buick and the Mustang, with her first job.

Later on, the children learned that they rather have Daddy punish them. Christee would always say, "I rather have my dad punish me for a lifetime because he will forget right away. My mom never forgets." He would issue an outrageous punishment and would forget about it within minutes, always with a smile and good disposition, and Christee was the same way.

My Christee's behavior was worrisome. Was Christee becoming an accident waiting to happen or a lucky girl?

I believe God had her in the palm of His hand and in his heart because He had a plan for her. But I don't think I knew that then, and believe me, I still struggle now with the same thoughts.

What was God's plan for Christee?

What was going on in our lives? Were we too busy to count our blessings and stop and notice that God was there helping us, guiding us, and warnings us? We worked, we attended church, loved our children, and spent time with them and the rest of the family. I was in the picture, but perhaps my mother was right; I was working too much and too hard.

Family was always first! Should I have stayed home?

I prayed then and cried today for Christee to forgive me if I did not spend as much time with her as she needed me.

Chapter 19

Asthma Attack!

Christee was shy of being four years old, almost a year without her getting into trouble or, should I say, major trouble.

She was growing but was very petite, and she was very cute and could almost get away with everything, and she went with me everywhere now.

We went grocery shopping, and while at the store, she said her chest hurt, and I could see that she was having trouble breathing, and I panicked. I remember going to the register and telling the clerk, mortified and embarrassed, that I needed to leave the store and couldn't wait to pay or put everything back on the shelves as my daughter was sick, and I needed to take her to the doctor. I didn't just want to abandon the shopping cart with the groceries, frozen food, and all. The clerk was so nice and understanding. A year later, during a parent conference at school, she recognized Christee and she asked how Christee was doing, so I went back to the same grocery store as I had stopped going because I was embarrassed that they thought I had been crazy, leaving all the food in the cart. Weird, that was me.

I got to Dr. Muney's office, and he immediately called for an ambulance. She was having an asthma attack.

I heard asthma, and I panicked. The lungs, the cystic fibrosis worries all over again.

Christee and I spent four days at Pioneer Hospital in Artesia. She was born at that hospital, and we were familiar with that hospital as it was our regular hangout by then. The hospital no longer exists, but my memories remain.

While at the hospital, the nurses were so gracious and enchanted by Christee and praised her as to how good she was; she never complained or cried when they took blood. The nurses were amazed when she told them that she "imagined it was like a little spider biting her." Not a big deal at all to her. She loved anything with more than two legs, whether insects or animals.

Whenever I took the kids for vaccinations, the nurses and I had to chase Davey around the office as he did not like getting those injections. After a while, Christee would tell Davey, "Close your eyes and just think it's an itsy-bitsy spider biting you." The baby sister, Christee, coaching the big brother on handling vaccinations; they loved and cared for each other so much, and the nurses used to laugh at how Christee was always calm about it.

As they grew older, she still tried to coach him in so many things, and he kept a watch on her and protected her. They were not twins, but they were loving brother and sister, and I was so happy to see them care for each other so much.

We were still at the hospital, figuring out what was wrong with Christee. Meanwhile, she developed an appetite; she was always a bad eater, so we were very happy to hear that she was hungry. One day, she told the nurse she wanted "broccoli soup and steak for dinner." The nurses laughed and explained the menu to her and left. However, later on when one of them went out to lunch, she brought Christee broccoli soup. What a kind and wonderful woman; she would not allow me to reimburse her, and Christee ate all the soup and forgot all about the steak but did ask for dessert.

The wheezing and coughing went away, and Christee was discharged with an asthma diagnosis and inhaler. All diagnostics went to her doctor.

Later a visit to her doctor revealed she had gained weight, was eating well, had no clammy hands, and had clean and clear lungs. We could all breathe a sigh of relief—at least for now!

I don't remember exactly how or when, but I know, I thanked you, Lord, and I praised your name. My child was okay.

Chapter 20

"I Want to Be a Veteran," She Announced

Christee was in the second grade when she came home all excited and announced she knew what she wanted to be when she grew up.

"A veteran. Yeah, that is what I want to do. I want to take care of all the animals in the world!" she said.

It took a while for us to understand and to make Christee understand that it was a *veterinarian* and not a *veteran*. "But my teacher said," she went on. She had such a drive and conviction even though she was so little that we knew she would someday be a veterinarian!

Between Christee and Davey, they found birds, cats, bunnies, chickens, turtles, and dogs, and she would nurse them back to health and find them homes. And yes, several funerals were had, and they were all buried on the side of the house; all those birds, turtles, and bunnies that did not make it.

Christee was healthy, other than a mild asthma, and she and Davey where taking music lessons, ice-skating, and gymnastics, and when Davey wanted to play accordion, she did too. Well, her brother was doing it, so why not her? She looked very funny holding the huge accordion; she was so petite. She loved to perform in school, and at home, whenever we had company, she was ready to sing or play the accordion.

When it came to singing, she was not shy at all. Sometimes, she waited until people asked her to sing, but if they didn't, she would certainly volunteer a song.

As she grew older, she would often say she would be a veterinarian first and then a singer. Her pets would always come first.

I didn't care much for pets, but the kids wanted them, and I always allowed them, thinking it would provide them with responsibility, kindness, and caring. Christee always took care of her pets and cleaned and fed them.

I remember one afternoon coming home from work and finding her crying and upset at Dustee Rose, the oldest of her dogs. I remember David laughing and making fun of her, telling her that Dustee was Nurse Ratchet from *One Flew Over the Cuckoo's Nest*.

You see, Christee had found Dustee thrashing a mouse and had intervened, saving the mouse from Dustee, only to find that the mouse had a broken leg. Christee had put a little piece of wood on the leg, as a splint, but ran out of tape, so she had told Dustee, "Don't touch it. Keep an eye on it," and she went into the house to get more tape. When she came back, the mouse was dead. She put Dustee on time-out, picked up the mouse's remains, and went in the house, crying.

She had a kind heart and loved animals. I had a serious talk with her about mice.

I do not remember when she wrote a rolodex card and put it in my rolodex. I found it one day as I was looking for a card.

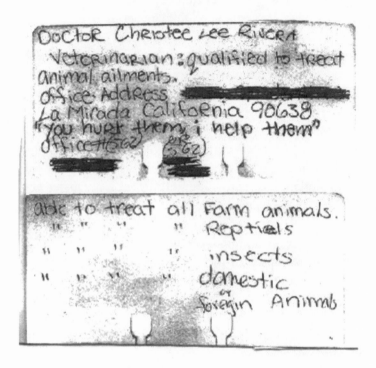

I cried when I came across this rolodex, her handwriting, her enthusiasm of someday being a veterinarian, her love for animals; I cried because I know now that . . . it would never be.

Chapter 21

Writing Sad Songs

Life went on, and it was good. Christee loved to sing and began to write songs.

My mother died when I was born.
My father left a short time after,
and me and my brother are all alone.

These are some of the lyrics of one of her songs. I would tell her to write happy songs, and she would say, "Sadness comes easier to me."

She sang Patsy Cline's song "Crazy" and Kris Kristofferson's "Sunday Morning," and in Spanish, she sang Linda Ronstadt's "Dos Arbolitos" and "Los Laureles," and she sang with such passion and feeling for the words and storyline. Everyone would tell us that those songs were not for children, but David sang them, and Christee learned them and loved to sing them.

She kept a notebook where she wrote so many songs. I am sorry I did not know about music nor took the time to learn it with her. I have not yet found her book—well, may be I should say, I have not yet been able to go through all her personal things. It still hurts too much to go in her room and look through her personal belongings.

Could it be self-preservation? I am scared to look through her things. At times I feel that she is owed her privacy; they are her things. The emotions and feelings in me are so hard to control that I choose the easiest way, and I tell myself, "LATER."

I pray for the day that I can go through her room and just reminisce on all the times we spent together there and be able to look through her things without crying or being angry or having that question in my mind again, *Why, Lord?*

I hope I find her notebook where she wrote so many sad songs, yet she always had that big smile and was ready to sing you a song. She was a happy child.

Chapter 22

Determination

I told you Christee was focused and determined in what she wanted, from the day she announced she wanted to be a veterinarian to the day she announce she wanted to go to Fullerton High School. Not in our district and not that close to our home either.

David and I had discussed and agreed that the children would go to a public high school. We had provided them with the foundation of a Catholic school education, and if they really wanted to learn and excel, they would do it from a public school.

Davey attended La Mirada High School, but Christee announced that she wanted to go to Fullerton High School. She had researched it, and they had very strong programs on choir/music and on agriscience.

She asked me to call and set up an appointment to go and meet with the director of the program and for a tour of the farm. I remember calling and setting up the appointment on a hot day, in the early afternoon. I figured it would be dirty and smelly with all the animals they had—and I hoped she would not like it.

We walked in, and I wanted to throw up. I was ready to leave the place, and Christee calmly said, "It smells good, just like a real farm. I want a farm when I become a veterinarian. Mom, I'm going to love it here."

Once she heard that she would get to raise an animal and take it to the Orange County Fair to compete, there was no way she was going to change her mind.

The choir director loved her voice and told her about the required discipline, frequent afterschool performances, and grueling practice for competitions, and she was so excited and not afraid of any of it.

The next few weeks, I tried to dissuade her; she would leave her friends, she would have to get up extra early to feed her animal, clean the stable, and get to her zero period on time. Truth is, I did not want to have to get up any earlier to take her to school, and what about Davey? He would either have to walk or run the risk of getting to school late if I did not make it back on time. And what about in the afternoon? How would she get home?

And no matter what I said, she found a way and would not let it go.

Special district permits were needed, and I applied for them. I was very angry when it was denied, and Christee cried because she wanted to be in those programs and our local school did not have them. Yes, I had tried to persuade, influence, and talk her out of going to Fullerton, but now, seeing her disappointment, I knew I had to fight the district.

She was so thrilled when they finally gave us the permit. She would say, "I know I am going to miss my friends, but I'll get to have my animals."

She went to Fullerton High and raised lambs for four years. My mother had discouraged her from getting pigs and steers. She competed and won some awards. And I saw her take care of those animals, even the ones that were not hers.

I remember one time, she came home very late and very tired, and she went straight to the shower and then to bed. "I am so tired," and she named some of her classmates in the agriculture science class. "They don't care about their animals. They haven't bought feed nor have they cleaned their stalls, Mom. It's so sad, those poor animals. I went and cleaned out their stalls and gave them fresh water and food from my lamb. I am not doing homework tonight. I am tired." And she fell asleep.

That scene repeated itself so many times, but I had learned not to argue anymore when it came to her animals.

In the fifth grade, Christee had developed allergies, and the doctor had told me to get rid of all her stuffed animals and to keep her away from cats. Well, we had two kittens at that time; one was hers, and the other, her cousin Nancy's. They had convinced me to get them cats, but my sister had not agreed to it, so we gave Nancy's cat room and board. And when the doctor said to keep her away from it, she was very upset and told me, "What if the doctor told you, 'Mrs. Rivera, you are allergic to Christee,' and would you get rid of me?" She had a response and a way to everything. I told her I would not get rid of her but would find her a home where they would take good care of her, and they would allow me to visit her once in a while. She found the cats a home and did visit for a while.

Chapter 23

Absentminded!

Did I mention that Christee was also known for her absentmindedness? Well, at times, and if it did not involve her animals or her singing, she would forget to tell us or do something important like get money for the bus or take a jacket or an umbrella.

She didn't have to walk a mile to go to school or in the rain because I dropped her off every day by six in the morning. But she did have to take the bus from school to her Nina Jeannette Arellano's house and wait there until either David or I could pick her up, and sometimes, we were late. It was very hard and difficult for everyone including the Arellanos who were nice to have her stay there every day after school for a whole year and then some.

The rainy season, not much in California, came, and she would often forget to get money for the bus, and she would have to walk in the rain and carry a huge load of books. Yes, she was stubborn too as, many times, I suggested a backpack with wheels, but it was "not cool," so she would rather carry the backpack. She did not complain and was happy singing and raising her lambs.

When she was invited to be in the honors class, she did not tell us. I found out from a letter she showed me weeks later; she declined. "My friends will think I am not cool."

She wanted to be liked, be "cool," whatever that really means, and most of all, she wanted to have fun and was not afraid of working hard for what she wanted. She looked fragile; her body was fragile, but her heart was so strong, and her convictions, even more so, and she stayed in the agriculture science and music programs for four years and earned honors in both classes.

Chapter 24

At the Steering Wheel Again!

"You will not drive until you're forty years old." Remember the punishment David had given her after she crashed the Buick? Well, David had forgotten all about. After all, his punishments were always welcomed by the kids. They were so outrageous that you just knew he wasn't serious about them.

Davey and Christee were ready to drive. They took driver's training and then we allowed them to drive us everywhere we went for them to acquire as much experience as possible. After a year of driving with us, Christee got a car.

Davey is the oldest, but it was Christee that got the car first. It was a necessity. Although they did not complain, it was hard on everyone: Davey was home from school alone, and Christee was at the Arellanos' after having to walk and take the bus to their house after school. It was decided Christee would start driving first. I would often remind her she still owed us for the repairs to the Mustang she had crashed with the Buick, and therefore, she could not afford to get herself in another car accident. "Be courteous and be safe, and may God bless you." It was my blessing to my children every morning when they left for school, college, or anywhere else they went.

It was so nice to get up, make breakfast for the kids, wave good-bye to Christee and then go and take Davey to school and come back home to leisurely drink my coffee before I went to work. I had time for myself! Yet I missed driving Christee. You see, she sang all the way to school, most of the time, while putting her make up on, or she would tell me about the chorale/choir competitions and the drama at the farm. But it was so nice in the evening, coming home and smelling the cookies or cakes that Christee loved to bake.

She was so responsible for some things and so irresponsible for others. She had asked David to teach her to change a flat tire in case something happened, and he did. Although we had given her the Triple A card, she kept a flashlight and pencil and paper in the glove compartment in case she was in an accident, and she needed to take notes of the other driver. But she would often, at night, remember that she had forgotten to put gas, and David would get up and go put gas in the car. She studied so hard; it did not come easy for her. She really had to discipline herself to get good grades, and she did.

Chapter 25

Asthma Again!

She was in the tenth grade when she came home late one day, and she walked in coughing and complaining that her chest hurt. She was tired and cold. Did I mention she was stubborn? I remember telling her to go lie down and rest, but she complained she had so much homework and went to take a shower and then sat down to do her homework and kept on coughing. I went and sat next to her and put some Vicks on her back and rubbed it down. She had no fever, and I knew it would warm her up, and it did.

After a few days with the same cough, I took her to the doctor. A quick chest and back exam and he declared it was "winter asthma." The doctor prescribed an inhaler and said to her, "Stay warm." She hardly ever wore a sweater.

I often called the Doctors' Exchange at night to ask if I should take her to emergency because of her persistent coughing at night, and he would say, "No need. Give her an extra puff of the inhaler," or would prescribe another type of inhaler and a cough medicine.

She would be fine in the morning, and off to school she went but not without first warming up her voice and waking up whoever was still asleep. She really loved to sing!

Winter asthma, cold mornings, or cold evenings, she would come in and I would rub Vicks on her back and chest, and she would stop coughing and fall asleep. The spring and summer came, and the cough would be gone, and another year went by. We worried, but when the weather got warm, she was fine, and the cough went away.

Chapter 26

Sweet Sixteen!

Her fifteenth birthday was fast approaching, and I wanted to celebrate it big with a *quinceañera* celebration, but she wouldn't have it; she wanted a sweet sixteen instead and nothing big.

I remember telling her, "Good. One more year to save and plan I could have a bigger celebration." And then she said, "What? Mom, whose party is it going to be—yours or mine?" I remember saying, "Well, it's a family event." And she said, "Okay, a family event, but not your party or all your friends that I don't know, and they don't know me and will bring me a gift that they had a hard time picking because they don't know me, or they'll give me money because they don't know what I like. No, I don't want a party like that. I don't want anything at all." She was stubborn, and I knew that.

After a couple of days, I went back to her and said, "Okay, it is your birthday. What is it that you want?" She was all excited and said, "I have the right place. Angelo's and Vinci's, they have real good pizza and spaghetti and are not that expensive." That was my Christee, and that was where she wanted her sweet sixteen party, and I said okay. She wanted a princess theme and wanted to make a list of the guests. "The people that know me and saw me grow up. Of course, the immediate family will be invited." They did know her after all! But she wanted her friends, and those that saw her grow up.

I was so proud of her when she showed me the guest list. I started asking who some of the people were, and I was a bit embarrassed that I did not know some of them as much as she did and as much as she made them part of her life. The pool man, Mike. "He saw me grow up and even helped me to learn to swim better. I see him and talk to him every week. He is a must, Mom." And then she named the neighbors that I barely knew, but she and Davey always talked to them, and she wanted them there too. She had such a big heart and was so considerate of people and their feelings.

Because a quinceañera celebration includes a religious aspect to it, like having a Mass at church, and Christee knew that I had been looking forward to it, she pointed out that Deacon Art and Mary Helen, from our church, were in her list and that maybe Deacon Art could give her a blessing.

The list grew with my guest, but she trimmed it down in order to have it at the place she wanted. Yes, they were my friends who knew of her but did not know her, and she reminded me that we had a deal: *it was her party.*

The party was in August, before school started. She was very excited, and I remember she kept singing a song. I didn't know the name of the song then, but she would sing it and play the guitar and then one day, she approached David and asked him if he could play the guitar for her at the celebration while she sang "I Could Not Ask for More" by Edwin McCain.

> *Lying here with you, listening to the rain.*
> *Smiling just to see a smile upon your face.*
> *And these are the moments I'll remember all my life.*
> *I found all I've waited for and I could not ask for more.*
> *Looking in your eyes, seeing all I need.*
> *Girl, I think you are it's everything to me.*
> *These are the moments I know heaven must exist*
> *These are the moments I know all I need is this.*
> *I have all I've waited for and I could not ask for more.*
> *I could not ask for more than this time together.*
> *I couldn't ask for more that this time with you*
> *Every breath has been answered.*
> *Every dream that has come through.*
> *Yeah, right here in this moment, it's that we're all meant to be.*
> *(Oh) here with you, here with me.*

And these are the moments I thank God that I'm alive.
And these are the moments I'll remember all my life.
I've got all I've waited for and I could not ask for more.
(Copied from MetroLyrics.com)

I remember never wanting to learn to play the guitar or knowing how to sing like I wish I did then so that I would spend all the time with her. To see them, David and Christee, laugh, sing, and then get serious when one of them messed up, it was like watching Christee when she was little and David teaching her how to sing, when he would tell her, "Breathe from your stomach," "You're off key," or "That was great." It was so beautiful!

The day of her party, she sang and danced with her father and with her Big Brother, and she was so happy. I remember seeing her go from table to table, thanking everyone for coming to her party and taking pictures with everyone at their table.

I was so happy she had put her foot down regarding the celebration. I didn't get to invite so many of my friends, and that part was hard and embarrassing, but after all was said and done, it was her party, and she enjoyed every minute of it.

I remember, prior to the celebration, pulling out old pictures and videos, wanting to put one together of all the years, one that would allow us to live back those memories of the children growing up. We ended up getting a professional one done for us by Christee's *nino*'s brother. I want to see that video again so bad that it pains me—my inability to go and look for it . . . What if it's not in her room? I have not found it in the house. All that remains is for me to look for it in her room. Her privacy or my fear, what is it that I am afraid of?

And I pray that someday I have the strength to look for it, find it, and THEN . . . to be able to watch it. But not now. It hurts too much. When will it go away? Dear God, will the pain ever go away?

Chapter 27

A New School Year

With every school year, we knew there would be a challenge. A new animal to be bought for the farm, a whole bunch of performance dresses, and yes, perhaps a new boyfriend, one she might take seriously and put the books away for. Dave and I joked that "September is coming, and we should embrace and see what Christee has in store for us."

We feared what September would bring but never imagined what a September would take, not then.

This particular year was a singing tour in Europe. She came home so excited that the new choir teacher had told them they would go representing Southern California, and she announced, "I am going no matter what." Yes, I was a bit overprotective, and I didn't let my children go anywhere unless I went with them or I knew the family she would go with, and she knew this. "They'll be fund raising, and I am going to need money. Can you give me a job at your office?" And we knew there was no stopping her. She would work hard, and she would go!

Around November, as the weather was getting a bit colder, she began to tell me that she was very cold in the mornings while tending to her lamb, and her hands would get so cold they would "turn purple and would stay purple for a long time."

And all I could say to her was, "I told you to wash your hair at night, so that way, it is not wet in the morning when you leave. That is why you are cold." She laughed and said, "Mom, it's my hands, not my head." I bought her a pair a gloves the next day, and she laughed, "And I am going to clean the stable and the lamb with the wool gloves." I gave her a pair of yellow plastic dish washing gloves, and she laughed, and that was that.

I was so blind. Oh God, how is it that I did not see it? Shouldn't a mother just know?

In December of that year, 1999, while we were at the St. Paul of the Cross Christmas dinner celebration and listening to the band play, Davey, Christee, and I were all sitting next to each other. Davey was not feeling well but did not want to leave and miss the party and all. I saw Christee reach for her glass to take a drink of her soda, and I just couldn't believe what I was seeing, so I grabbed her hand, and I said, "What happened to your hand? Why is it purple?" She laughed and said, "I told you they get purple when I am cold."

It made no sense at all. We were all sitting in the Jinks Hall, not a very large hall, and there were many people. In fact, the room was warm; we had taken our jackets off. She felt warm and looked warm, all but her hands. They were cold—a cold that almost hurt when you touched her hands. I rubbed her hands with my own hands and held them against my chest, and all the while, she kept saying, "It's okay, Mom. It'll go away in a little bit as soon as I warm up." I blamed the fact that she was drinking soda with ice, and she said, "No, Mom. That is how they get every morning as soon as I leave the house even if my hair is not wet. They hurt a little, but don't worry. It goes away."

I got up and told them both, "Davey and Christee, get up. We are going to the emergency room." They were both upset, and Christee said, "Mom, you are exaggerating again. I am okay."

You see, when they were little, I took them to the doctor, and at times, I knew that, perhaps, it was nothing. I wanted the doctor to tell me so rather than me guess and be wrong, and I had a saying I used as they grew older and argued with me not to take them to the doctor. And the saying went like this: I rather have the doctor say, "There is nothing wrong with your children"—and that I exaggerated—"than have someone ask me, 'Señora, porque se murió su baby?'" (Lady, why did your child die?) and having to respond, "Porque no lo lleve al doctor" (Because I did not take him/her to the doctor).

My fears, my worst fears, and I took them to the hospital. Davey had a fever, and they took his jacket off and gave him some ice chips to cool him down. And Christee, they put her hands in warm water and gave her a warm blanket, and they ran tests, and they brought other doctors in to see her, and they were all talking. Christee had a smile, and they, my kids, were making fun of me to "change the Nina face," worried expressions shown on my face like my own mother made when she was worried.

"Raynaud's syndrome," one doctor said. "Yes, I think that's what she has, and it is due to cold temperatures, but you need to take her to her doctor for more tests." And he gave us paperwork and sent us home. Davey was feeling better, his fever had gone down, and Christee's hands were warm again as they kept giving me blankets to keep her warm. And we went home.

On Monday morning, Christee went to school like nothing had happened, and I called her doctor's office for an urgent appointment. I also called a friend of mine, who is a doctor. I told him what happened and what they told me, and he said, "Don't worry about it. California is a warm-weather state. If you lived in cold weather, then I would tell you to move. Do make sure they test her for lupus."

What? What is lupus?

Oh God, here we go again! Are you here with Christee?

After testing and second opinions, it was confirmed; she had lupus and Raynaud's syndrome. There was no family history of any of that in either side of the family, but Christee had it, and we were all so afraid for the future, Christee's future. But Christee kept her smile, and for days, she would say, "I have *lupitas*." And Davey and Dave would call her Lupita. It bothered me so much. How could they be so insensitive to her, but she would just say, "Stop, Mom. Don't work yourself up."

Chapter 28

Shopping, Searching, and Crying

My sisters and I went all crazy, shopping for matching gloves, scarves, sweaters, and cute socks. She didn't like anything nor did she want to wear them. "I don't want to look different. I don't want people to ask me anything." This time, she didn't smile, and she was almost angry.

Oh God, you gave me strength. I know you were there in that moment as I held my tears and replied.

"You won't be different. You will set a trend, and everyone will be wearing gloves, scarves, and hats. You'll be cool." I didn't want her to get cold or catch a cold. Her immune system was weak, and I needed to take care of her, but I needed her smile too, and it wasn't there, not this time.

Christmas came, and Christee got gloves, sweaters, socks, scarves, and hats. She was so polite and thanked everyone for the gifts, but her smile was not there, and I knew she was not my happy child anymore.

At home, she lost it; she was so angry and upset with me that I had told the family of her illness because now everyone was "feeling sorry for me." I told her no one was feeling sorry for her. They loved her and cared for her, but she was upset and did not want to listen to what I had to say, and I knew we had to do something and soon.

I scheduled counseling for the family. We all needed help to learn to deal with the situation and, more importantly, for Christee. I didn't want to lose her smile, happy-go-lucky attitude, and her love for singing and LIFE!

It didn't go well. She didn't want to hear about it. In fact, she was angry and rebellious and flatly said NO.

My memory fails me here. I do not remember the date, or maybe, I don't want to remember when it happened, but it was shortly after the counseling discussion that, in the middle of the night, around two in the morning, Davey came to our room and woke us up and told us that he had heard a noise in Christee's room and woke up. But after a while, he went to the bathroom and checked on her, and she was gone. Her room was empty, and he had already looked throughout the house. The car was there, but Christee was gone.

He found a note. Although young, Davey knew her well and was so hesitant to show us the note, but he did.

The note went something like this: "Don't look for me, and don't call the pigs to look for me." We were stunned!

Dear God, please protect my baby. We knew she was not well. She would never call anyone a pig; she respected the police. She was lost and all alone in the middle of the night, and it was cold. I prayed while David called the police.

It was so embarrassing when the officers read her note. We had raised our children to be loving, caring, and respectful, yet her words didn't just show disrespect but such unkind and hurtful words. We knew it was not Christee that wrote the note but her pain and anger that overwhelmed her senses.

The officers were so polite and understanding once we told them about her recent diagnosis and no previous problems or history of running away. We didn't know how long she had been gone; Davey thought a half hour at the most from when he heard a noise. They asked if she had a history of hurting herself and told us how critical it was for her to be found immediately.

Hurt herself? *Oh God, please be with her. That was all I could think of.*

I called a few of her friends that lived closed by, and no one had seen her or heard from her. I was told to stay home in case she came back, and David and the police went out and drove around looking for her.

I cried and cried, and I asked God to protect her to watch over her, to keep her safe, and to let me see her smile again.

Around five in the morning, they found her! She was sitting on a park bench. They had already gone by there a few times, but they had not seen her as it was dark and the bench was close to one of the buildings, but they found her. She was cold and scared.

She was safe!

Dear God, thank you for bringing my child back! Was she really back?

Chapter 29

The Europe Singing Tour

In January, she told us she no longer wanted to go to Europe on the singing trip. We knew right away that she was afraid of getting sick and us not being there with her.

Although she was doing better, after family counseling and individual counseling for her understanding and dealing with her illness, the smile was not quite back nor the daring and fearless Christee. We needed her back. We always told her, her future was up to her, and her decisions, actions, and character would define her. She was definitely afraid of making decisions.

Her character and work ethic intact, she got up without problems and went to school, tended to her animals, and went to choir class, practice, and performances, but Christee's heart was not into anything at all.

We were also getting her a specialist for lupus, which is a rheumatologist. Forgive me, but I cannot even write his name now without getting anxious and angry, so I will omit his name but tell you he was well recommended by various people, and I did in fact check his standing with the Medical Quality Assurance office. How is it that he failed her and when he did, we'll talk about later, not now.

He was nice to Christee and even told us he had a daughter that was Christee's age. She felt comfortable with him, and he became her doctor.

She didn't like the medicines she was given. They made her tired and sleepy and "They don't let me do all the things I need to do," she would say, and the doctor would change them, and after awhile, she was feeling good but still not wanting to go on the trip.

I reminded her how much she wanted to go before her illness and how hard she had worked to raise some of the money and how I had paid the deposit. I would often say, "You are going on the trip."

One day, when I saw that she had totally given up on the trip, I was angry at her, and I told her, "I didn't raise a quitter. You are fine to travel. We'll speak to the doctor and the medical insurance to be sure you are covered while you are traveling. If you get sick, you'll call the doctor, and if need be, you come back early, or I'll go and meet you up there. That's the last I want to hear about that." She was crying, and I walked away.

I was so afraid to let her go on the trip. I was afraid to push her too hard, but I knew that if I held her back or allowed her to hold herself back, she would never be the outgoing and vibrant person that she was before, and her smile would never be there again. I needed to be strong for her and encourage her, and I did even when my heart was hurting, and all I wanted was to hold her and tell her, "Mom and Dad are here for you. You don't have to go anywhere if you don't want to." But I didn't.

Her doctor told her she was fine to travel and gave her his phone number and told her he was only a phone call away while she was in Europe and encouraged her to call anytime if she was feeling sick.

Her choir practices got more demanding, and the new animal was coming in; I had no choice but to help her with her animals and the farm duties. I had always been a very supportive parent, but now I needed to be more hands-on and began to go and help her with the lamb on the weekends. Dave helped too, and little by little, we began to see her coming back, especially once the weather began to warm up. No more close-toed shoes with heavy socks and gloves. No more purple hands and feet.

Chapter 30

Her Smile and Song Were Back!

It started in junior high when she wanted braces, the "first phase." She didn't have all her baby teeth out, but she kept saying she wanted beautiful teeth to go with her smile, so I caved in.

It wasn't until her senior year that the braces came out. She was tired of them, and we all made fun of her. Of course, throughout those years, we had to pay extra for the braces to be removed and then put back for some of the "special pictures or performances."

I won't ever forget the day she came from the dentist without her braces for good. She wouldn't stop seeing herself in the mirror and showing us her teeth and thanking both Dave and I for paying for her dentist; she was so appreciative, and her face was glowing with happiness.

"I look like a big girl now. Not like a little girl, huh, Mom." Wittily I responded, "You need to act like a big girl too, Christee. Stop with the mirror already." And we all laughed at her. She was wearing jeans, a T-shirt, tennis shoes, and her hair was parted with braids hanging on each side of her face; she did not look any older than a thirteen-year-old.

She was once again confident and daring but had already told us that she would not pursue out-of-state college. She would rather stay close to home.

My heart once hurt so much hearing her tell me, "I am going to apply to all the colleges away from California, away from you. You have to cut the strings, Mom," while motioning her fingers like a scissor. Now my heart hurt differently. I was sad not because of me but because I knew she was *now* afraid to be on her own.

She won a few of the Orange County Fair competitions with her lambs; she worked hard and had not lost her vision to become a veterinarian. I tried to encourage her to apply to out-of-state colleges, even out of the country, but she decided to stay close to home.

We, of course, went through the drama of the senior pictures and the class ring. Yes, hundreds of dollars for the pictures, and she did not like any of them after we bought them. We ended up going to the mall and getting her a $14.99 package that she liked, displayed, and gave to friends.

The class ring—oh God, we argued about it. She was known to misplace jewelry, her own and mine. I knew she would only wear it for a little bit and then either lose it or not want to wear it, and I was firm and said NO to the one she wanted.

I must have told my mother about the drama because she offered to buy Christee the ring, but Christee said no; she knew I would not allow her to buy the expensive one she wanted. After a while, my mother convinced me that we both should pay for it. That way, Christee would get what she wanted, and it would not cost either one that much. Christee promised to wear it all the time and not to lose it . . . right!

The ring had her name inside, *Christee* on the outside, the school mascot, and the music symbol on it too. Pricey, especially when I knew it would not last her that long.

The ring is priceless to me now, and I wear it proudly. She did lose it, and I will tell you about it later.

She had entered a song-writing contest with an antidrug song. And once again her sad songs came to life, and she enjoyed writing.

Realize
Christee Lee Rivera

We were all just a couple of friends
Hangin' around town
Smokin' joints and drinkin' beer
We all thought we down
Until a couple of guys moved in
Asked us who the hell are we foolin'
We thought we were cool
Never bothered with school
Tellin' jokes and gettin' high
We didn't realize
That all our hopes and dreams died
That all our time had passed us by
We always listen to you
And never listen to me
Oh Oh Oh
Oh Oh Oh
I've got to turn my life around
I've got to get some help
All of my friends I had
They all burned in hell
Now all my hopes and dreams died
Now all my time has passed me by
We thought we were cool
Never bothered with school
Tellin' jokes and getting' high
We didn't realize

The song placed in the contest!

The award was that she would record the song, and it would be marketed to high schools. She was so happy going to the recording studio to record her song. She asked Dave to go with her and borrowed his guitar. She played the guitar too while recording her song.

She came back from recording crying. The studio was very cold and her hands had turned purple, and the studio people "freaked out," as she put it. They were scared and wanted to stop the recording and reschedule. She didn't like people to look at her differently or treat her differently.

"Christee, did you cry at the recording?" I asked. "No, Mom. I asked for a break and went to the bathroom and ran the hot water over my hands. They warmed up, and I was okay. I went back to finish the recording."

I wonder whatever happened to the song/recording? I mean, we have a copy, but I don't know what the Department of Education did with it.

I did care; I just didn't know how to go about her singing career and she always said that "if I was in the middle of a concert singing and they told me one of my animals needed me, I would leave the concert to help my puppies."

She graduated high school with honors in both music and agriscience. She had been accepted to Cal Poly Pomona and Fullerton State.

Christee was funny at times and yet very serious at other times. She had been approached by a sorority at Cal Poly Pomona. When we had gone to the open house, she was so excited about it until she heard some of the girls talking about another girl and saying, "Let's invite the other girl too. She is cute and has a nice smile." She later told us that she didn't want to belong to a group of girls, "so shallow."

She opted for Cal State Fullerton even though she really liked the program at Cal Poly Pomona. "It will be closer and cheaper, Mom." I said nothing. There were so many times that I just kept quiet. I did not want to push her more than she pushed herself. She carried the illness, she carried the burden, and I could not help her with her fears or feelings of not having control of that illness.

A Caribbean cruise for her graduation and her eighteenth birthday, we knew that it was probably the last time that Davey and Christee would want to go on vacation with us, and we planned to celebrate their birthdays on a cruise. We were so excited, and even other family members decided to go on the trip with us.

Christee was focused on college now and had applied to a summer program at Cal State Fullerton after deciding that she would go there. She discovered that the trip was going to "interfere" with her school schedule, and she decided that her school was more important. I kept saying "It's only two days you will miss from school," and she kept saying, "Even one day is too many." She did not go with us on the trip; she was not afraid of being alone once again, and that we treasured.

My child was indeed back, and Dave and I knew that September was around the corner again. We had to be vigilant with her. What could we expect this September?

Oh, and the ring. Before the end of summer, she had lost it. I had her go to my mother's and tell her about losing the ring.

Chapter 31

Trouble Again

She began to complain about her doctor: how he was always booked and it was hard to get the appointment and then she would wait two to three hours at the office. But she would then say, "But he is nice, and I am doing well. I guess I'll stay there."

Occasionally, I would insist for her to let me go with her. She was over eighteen then, and when I did go, I complained about the wait and would speak to the office administrators, and they would apologize always, saying, "You know, he is so nice and good with the patients that's why the long wait and the delay." Christee would be mad at me for complaining and would not let me go with her again for a while.

"Her lupus is fine and controlled. She is doing well." That was her doctor's answer anytime I called or when Christee went for checkups.

She seemed fine, but we started to see that she was not eating well. She actually had a great appetite but would complain of stomach pain anytime she ate. She snacked all day and was hungry all day. Visits to the doctor were more frequent for her stomach pain, and medicines for her stomach began to take over, and she hated medicine and being sick.

She had a smile but began to be moody and rebellious as when she was younger and began to get into trouble, and we were concerned.

The focus on her studies began to dwindle; she began to go out and come home late. She would say, "I am over eighteen, and I can do what I want," and she said it with conviction and anger. I didn't like that, and I was afraid she would quit school and afraid of her losing the health insurance through us if she was not enrolled in school but more afraid that she would go astray or become someone she wasn't.

We had given the children a good upbringing, one with principles and respect for each other, and she was not being *thoughtful about any of that.*

She wanted me to say yes to everything she wanted even when it was not in her best interest, and I refused. Yes, she had an illness, an incurable disease, but just like I did not allow that illness to make her a handicap, I refused to let that illness make her brazen, disrespectful, and uncaring for herself or her family, and I told her so.

I remember praying and asking God to guide me and help me make the right decision, and I told David I was going to have a conversation with the children (eighteen and nineteen years old) and asked him to just listen, and if he disagreed with me, I would give him an opportunity to say so but that he should wait until then so they would not undermine my position, and he agreed.

I sat both Davey and Christee down and David too and told them that belligerence and blatant behavior was not to be tolerated. That while they were under our roof, they were to follow rules and discipline, and if they did not like what was expected of them and were not willing to respect the house rules, they would have to leave. I also explained to them their need for health insurance and education and that both went together in order for their father and me to continue to support both of them. I told them that those were my rules and my guidelines, and I was willing to support their education and health insurance as long as they followed the rules.

I also told them that I did not speak for their father and that it was his house too and that he could overrule me if he wanted, but I needed a decision from them before David said anything and that they should think it over and carefully.

Christee immediately said she would rather leave. I think Davey had to leave too in order to be in solidarity with his sister. His behavior was not really a problem, but he had chosen to put a ring on his tongue, and I would not stand for that.

Both of them left the house as my husband had stood by me and simply said, "Mom is right, and you two cannot divide us because one day you will both leave anyway, and Mom and I will be left alone."

I was so heartbroken; I never thought they would leave. I thought they would be unsettled and follow the rules for a few weeks and then we would rehash the conversation, and at one point, they would just outgrow that stage and life would be happy again. But not this time!

Dear God, what did I do?

I still think of that phase of our lives, and I regret it so much, but I must tell you, Christee and I discussed this passage of our lives several times, and I will share that with you later.

My poor husband, I had placed him in such a horrible position, and now he had to suffer with me. We were sad and lonely.

My mom, relatives, and friends would later tell me to "let them be" and that it was a stage all kids went through. "Christee is sick. Don't be too hard on them. They are good kids." Yes, they were good kids, and that was what I was trying to preserve and safeguard, their character and their love and respect for family. And yes, Christee was sick but still needed to know right from wrong, and it was my duty as a mother to help her see that, right?

May God forgive me for what I put the family through.

Chapter 32

Stubbornness!

A whole year went by, and Christee and Davey were gone.

I saw Davey often enough; he moved in with Grandma and Grandpa and went to East Los Angeles College, and I knew he was okay. I talked to my mother-in-law every day; they were so happy having him with them, but they had been upset about the whole thing too.

Christee was a different story. I was angry at her more so than Davey. He at least had told me he was leaving and where he was going but not her, not even a good-bye.

How could I have been so blind I put the whole family in such a position!

Once we found out where she was, I would have David call and be sure she was fine and kept up current with her doctor's appointments, medicines, and schooling. I would see her at Mom's house or any of the family gatherings, and I would not speak to her. Just thinking about it, my heart aches as much as it hurt then for being so stubborn and not talking to her, or was it her that was stubborn in not coming back?

Dear God, who in their right mind would have done that?

She would often call, and I would pick up the phone and hear her voice, and my heart would jump with joy only for my voice to then say, "Wait, I'll call your father." Dave would pick up the phone and ask all the questions I had told him to ask her: How are you feeling? Did you take your medicine? Did you eat? Do you have money for food? Do you need anything for school? And I would be there next to him to listen to her voice and reassure myself that she was fine.

What a horrible mother I had become.

One day, Christee told Dave she wasn't feeling well and complained to Dave that she would, at times, miss the doctor's appointment because she would get tired of waiting; the two—to three-hour wait was now three to four hours, and she complained to the nurses, but they didn't pay attention to her.

I would call the insurance and complained and threatened to change doctors, but Christee liked him, and he was "controlling the lupus." And she stayed on with him.

Davey and Christee had bank accounts since they were babies, and they tapped into them. The money was theirs after all. I didn't know when, but they both ran out of money. Christee got a part-time job but was tired and was having trouble keeping up with her school and doctor's appointments, and Dave and I were worried she would stop school, and the insurance would not cover her. Davey was okay, living with the grandparents.

One day, Dave told Christee to talk to me, to come back, to make it easy on herself, but she was afraid. "Mom won't want to. She doesn't speak to me." Dave convinced her to come home and talk to me about coming back and following the house rules.

Funny, Christee had commented to Dave that they were not bad after all and that she kind of understood why there were rules to be followed. "My roommates leave wet towels on the bathroom floor and tooth paste all over the sink. It's gross," and "There is never any food in the refrigerator since I ran out of money. It's horrible, Dad."

I remember crying when he told me how much she missed us or the security of the home, and I was sad for her and happy for me. She would come back. I knew Davey would come back too if she was back. My heart was joyous and apprehensive.

Christee came to talk to me, and David was present, and she apologized and asked to be allowed to come back.

Dear God, you know I wanted to hug her and kiss her and tell her it was all right. She could come back, and I didn't even care about the house rules anymore.

But my stubbornness, I found out, would not let me do that. Instead I questioned her, "Why would you want to be back? It's the same mother 'who doesn't understand.' The same house with all the rules."

I told her how proud I was of her that she could make it on her own and that she had shown character in standing for her rights and beliefs, and that was what I always wanted her to do, always.

I was not trying to break her, for indeed, I was proud of her. I would have never gone out of the house without my mother's permission, let alone go against mother's rules. Christee was strong again, and I knew she had conquered that lack of self-confidence and fear that she had developed when she was first diagnosed with lupus. No more self-pity or "wrong attention needed."

I thanked God for finally giving me my daughter back, spirit and smile.

And I welcomed her back. I hugged her and told her how much I loved her, and Dave went to pick up her stuff. What a wonderful day that was.

Thank you, God!

Davey was ready to come back too. Unfortunately, the situation at my in-laws had changed, and I felt compelled to have Davey stay with my mother-in-law. She needed him now, and he stayed. My son has always had a kind and compassionate heart and loved his *gemita*.

Chapter 33

Christee as a Coworker

Davey and Christee wanted to work but couldn't find a job that was flexible with their school schedules, and for Christee, it was even harder as she had several doctor's appointments every month, so they asked if they could work for me again, like they did every summer during high school, and I agreed. They would do their homework first and then they would help out with specific duties.

But they had no idea that they were tapping on the same money I usually gave them or paid the college tuition with. At times, I ended up without any spending money for myself after I paid rent, office expenses, and them, but I was happy having them there with me.

They each had their workstation, and I tried to give them challenging work rather than just photocopying or filing assignments. I remember having a talk with Christee about office procedures, responsibilities, and learning to share with coworkers knowledge and supplies. She had labeled everything including the trashcan with her name as "Belonging to Christee." Years later, those labels were painfully removed.

Davey was especially good with computer programs I bought for the office, and he would figure them out and then teach me and Christee how to use them.

Christee had chosen a workstation that faced the window to my private office, and at times, I would have to tell her, "Stop talking. I need to do some work if you want to get paid." She would come from school and tell me what she learned or what her frustrations were. She would also ask me, "How do you know which is the right guy for you?" or ask, "How did you know dad was the right guy for you?"

She had had her share of boyfriends. We were not happy with anyone, but we tried to be nice. We did not want to alienate her, and she wanted to find the "special guy" for her life. We knew that her illness was always in the back of her mind or, perhaps, present at all times like it was in our lives, Dave's and mine's. She wanted to live life in a hurry!

We would talk about her becoming a veterinarian and traveling the world before she found the "right guy" and how she wanted me to be her office manager and be sure everyone did their work.

She wanted to buy a ranch where she could build kennels to board pets, build a pet hospital and her clinic, and have her house there too. She would say, "Animals all around, and you won't be able to say anything to me because I'll be your boss. Would you work for me?" And I would say, "Yes, Christee, but for now, finish your homework and let me work for us to pay the tuition this quarter."

She would talk about her Europe trip and ask if we would pay for her to go to Africa on a safari after she finished her undergraduate work, and I would say, "Yes, Christee, if we can just do the work right now, I may be able to save for your trip." She would quiet down and do her work but only for a while until I would get serious and ignore her.

It was so nice to have someone at the office, most of the time, and when it came time for me to go on vacation, I didn't have to close the office as I usually did. Christee agreed to be responsible for messages and paperwork. Only what attorneys knew, she normally processed. Davey agreed to help if Christee needed it. By then, he had found a part-time job; I had fired him for talking back to his boss—ME!

When I came back from vacation, I found out that she had done such a good job that she had been offered a job close to home by one of the attorneys that gave me work! I was proud of her and sad for me. No more talking about her future plans or what went on during her day at school. I would have to wait until I got home. She was very excited, and again, I was proud.

Chapter 34

New Friends!

Christee loved her work and met very nice people there. They were flexible with her work schedule, and she continued going to school, dropping classes at times because she was not feeling well.

She was tired, and at times, she would say, "Forget about being a veterinarian, Mom. I'll just go for vet tech." And my heart would ache. I knew she was tired, and her health was frail, and I would tell her, "Whatever you want, Christee. Is it going to make you happy?" And she would, at times, respond no, and at times, she would respond, "I am tired." And the next day, she would get up and go to school. Yes, she had been attending college for a while and had to drop classes at times because of asthma flare-ups, joint pain, stomach pain, and other stomach problems.

She had new friends at the office and also at home. She began hanging out with Davey and his friends, which she had not done for a while. They had both gone to different high schools and colleges. It was nice to see them go out. Christee would always be telling Davey, "Change shirt" or "Change pants" or "That doesn't go" or whatever, but it was heartwarming. They had grown up very close, and they were very close again.

One day, I found Christee looking through old pictures, her and Davey's birthday parties from their first birthday to about their fifth birthday. She made a mess. I asked what she was looking for, and she said she met this guy, and he said he knew her before, when she was little, and had come to our house for her birthday parties, but she couldn't remember him.

The new guy was Ramon, a nephew of one of my best friends, Ricardo Paz, from junior high and from a family I dearly care for. A new guy came into her life. Davey liked him. They had been friends when they were younger and had recently reacquainted, and Dave and I liked him too. He would probably not stop her from her dreams but encourage them.

She was happy, yet for the first time, I saw her unsure of herself and immature. I think back on those days, and I cry because I think she knew she was very sick and was afraid to fall in love. She was afraid that he was "the one" and that he would reject her because of her illness.

I once had a talk with her after having seen her from the window, arguing with him. I told her what love was; love was about trust, kindness, and unselfishness. I told her that if he was meant for her, she would not have to fight with him or for him and that jealousy made her look childish and insecure and that it was an illness, and she certainly did not want another illness, one that would certainly drive him away.

I reminded her how much I cared for him and his family and that I would not stand for her to hurt him. She cried as she lately did so often and promised me not to hurt him or the family that she now also cared for.

Oh God, I did not know what I was asking her, but she certainly meant not to hurt him. Dear God, why did he have to suffer too?

Chapter 35

Singing Again

Ah, it was nice to hear Christee sing and to see her pick up the guitar again. Ramon played guitar too, and they would get together and play music, and she had her "Christee smile" again. The songs were happier too.

Her stomach was hurting again—or still. She was not a complainer, so I never knew if it was again or just a continuous pain. New medicines, losing weight, gaining weight, eating, or not eating—it was such an up and down, but she was happy with her Ambo Beanba, as she called him and the love of her life as she later told us.

She always liked baking. Grandma Elsie had taught her, and she found out that her stomach didn't hurt when she ate cakes and cookies, and she began to bake even more. I remember coming home from a long day at work to the smell of freshly baked cookies. *How I long for that smell.*

It was around this time that she met a wonderful and courageous young woman who had lost her young son due to an asthma attack, and she told me the story and added, "I never knew asthma was that bad. I forget to carry my inhaler at times, and when I can't find parking close to my classes, I can barely breath. I get tired so fast."

I remember losing patience with her because she would not tell me these things as they were happening. She would not complain. I told her to call the doctor and demand that they do a breathing test and any other test necessary as it didn't sound right. "Mom, I had it done a few months ago, and he said all is okay. 'The lupus is dormant.' Don't worry."

She smiled and said, "Well, maybe I am just out of shape, but I'll ask for a new test so you won't worry and get mad at me." And then, just like nothing, "By the way, I got another parking ticket today."

Oh dear God, give me patience.

There were so many times that I just wanted to scream, or maybe I did. I would get so angry at her, but then I would see how hard she worked and her cute little smile, and my anger would go away but not without first issuing some kind of punishment or extra chores to pay for the parking ticket. She was a good driver, and other than parking tickets, there were no other type of infractions. Thank God for that.

My mother, who had been a disciplinarian all her life with all her children, now would tell me, "Just let it be. She is sick. You have no idea what she feels like." True, I had no idea of her thoughts or feelings, but I knew I didn't want to hear that she was sick, so I just stopped telling my mother whatever it was that was going on with Christee, unless of course it was something good that we could celebrate so my mother would not worry.

Chapter 36

Halloween 2004

A HOLIDAY! Thank God, NOT one that is a weekend celebration, not one where the family gets together. Everyone on their own, and so I thought, *I have nothing to worry about this holiday!*

On Sunday, October 31, 2004, Mom had called earlier in the day. She had changed her mind about getting together and shopping for a new car. "Maybe next weekend," she said. She was worried once again about one of her children, and I knew that.

As the evening started, I called and ordered a pizza before the trick-or-treaters started their parade. Davey and Christee had plans, so I knew it was going to be quite the night: Dave and I passing out candy and seeing the neighborhood kids and adults alike with their costumes and us taking the obligatory pictures.

The pizza had just arrived when the phone rang; it was Mom. There weren't the usual pleasantries or her usual "What are you doing? Should I call you later? Or call me when you are not busy." No, it was certainly not her usual phone call.

"*Mija*, it's happening again. It's the same headache I felt before. Come and take me to the doctor?" When Mom asked for something, you did not question it; you did it. She was never a complainer or one who imposed, demanded, or required her children to do anything for her. She always respected the fact that we had a spouse and children, and they came first, according to her, before the parents.

I knew it was bad for Mom to call me. I immediately told Dave to call 911 on the other phone while I called Mom's neighbor and told her to go over to her house. I was thirty minutes away without counting traffic.

I tried calling my sisters that lived closer to Mom, but they were not home. The 911 operator, after David gave her Mom's history, immediately called the paramedics and an ambulance to her house. The neighbor called while we were on route and said they were there and wanted to speak to me.

Once again, she was speaking gibberish, just like ten years before when she had had her aneurysm. The paramedic said they would send her to St. Francis Hospital, as it was the closest, and for me to meet them there.

I remember praying, but it was a different type of prayer. It was like I knew what was coming, and I was calm—a calmness that gave strength—but I was afraid, and all I remember was saying, *"Let it be Your will."*

I called my sister Ofie, you could always count on finding her at home, and I alerted her of the fact that "It's happening again. All over again with Mom." And she knew what I was talking about. "Call the others. I will be at St. Francis." Dear God, someone had to call Maggie in San Diego and go to Tijuana to pick up Dad. He had just left the day before.

I remember having the presence of mind or the sense to say "Don't tell Maggie Mom is in the hospital. She had just had a baby, and Mom would not want her to be frightened. It would affect the baby." I am sure that would have been Mom's concern and worry.

Dave and I got to the hospital as the ambulance attendants were bringing her into the emergency room.

I saw Mom on the gurney, and as I was walking toward her, she suffered a seizure. The ambulance attendants, who were still there, talking to the nurses about Mom's condition, immediately began working on her, and everyone was speaking, and I could not understand anything, but in my heart, I knew what was happening.

Did I have to witness that?

At times, when I close my eyes, I can almost see them both, Christee and Mom, in the same state, the same position, the same calmness surrounding them while pandemonium and chaos was happening all around them.

Even now my heart hurts when I think of that day, and the pain is so intense it feels like it's piercing my chest and is so deep it's so hard to breathe and then there is such an uncontrollable weeping that overcomes me, and all kinds of emotions rush through me: anger, anguish, and a wishful desperation that I am still asleep and dreaming.

But I am awake, and my body feels weak and frail, but on that day, I was strong—a strength that could only come from one place . . .

Was He there? I didn't think so then, but I do believe it now. He was there!

I was there, present and seeing them work fiercely for Mom's life. They intubated her, and they kept saying, "She is not responding." The nurse finally realized that I was there and took me out of the emergency room.

Mom went into a coma and died a few days later.

We celebrated her life and all of us thank God for "the miracle of those ten years." We were able to really appreciate her, and we saw the sacrifices she had made to give us, her children, a good upbringing and, above all, love.

Chapter 37

Reflection!

Mom had survived the aneurism she had suffered back in 1994 without ANY ill effects: no loss of memory and no paralysis or speech problems. The doctors and surgeons had told us they themselves thought Mom's life and recovery had been a miracle. We all still think that, and we thank God for those ten years He allowed us to enjoy Mom.

But on September 4, 2006, I found myself thanking Him that Mom was not there. You might think there must be something wrong with me. How can anyone in their right mind be glad their mother is gone?

Dear God, I was glad. Yes, I was glad Mom did not have to go through the pain.

My world, my happiness, my song was gone. What happened?

I needed Mom there. I missed her then and now, but I was happy she had been spared the pain. Christee, oh dear God, Christee, what happened! I couldn't comprehend. I still wake up, wanting to wake up.

Mom and I had grown so close, but I would not share with her my hardships. She had many of her own, and I knew I could not help her with her burdens. Why give her mine? So on that day, I would have not shared my burden with her.

When my heart is at peace, I reflect and thank God. Indeed, He had granted my mother the grace and favor to spare her life on that remote day in 1994. She had been a prayerful woman all her life. *Did He listen to her?* Or perhaps He heard the family as we had all prayed together with the most fervent faith, zeal, and heartfelt belief of His mighty power for her life—for a miracle.

Or had He answered me?

And will He hear me when I need Him again?

Chapter 38

My Comfort, My Children

Mom was gone. Who was going to listen to me now, and who was going to assure me that all was all right? Who was going to point out my mistakes or celebrate my accomplishments?

Davey was back at home. He could no longer help Elsie, my mother-in-law, by himself. Her children decided it was best for her to be at a nursing home. She had been a great mother-in-law to me and helped me with the children and always gave me good advice, yet there was nothing I could do for her but visit.

As the days went by, I remember just sitting and crying. I missed Mom very much, and I knew my sisters and brothers did too. There was no one I could call that would give me comfort.

Soon I realized that Christee was alert and paying attention to my needs, and when she heard me cry, she would immediately go in the room and find me and hug me. She would ask me, "Do you want to talk about it?" or would say "Tell me about Nina when she was young."

At the time, I couldn't speak but would cry more and hold her tight, and she would say, "It's okay. I am here for you now." She would stroke my back and then sit next to me until I stopped crying. I missed my mother so much, but I was so happy and glad my daughter was there to comfort me.

Davey would not say much, but he was there, and that was comfort too.

One of the times when I was crying and missing Mom so much, Christee and I just started talking, and I told Christee that Dustee Rose (Christee's oldest dog) had been there for me when Christee was gone. The whole year, when we were both being dumb and stubborn, Dustee had been my refuge and support then as she, Christee, was now. We both cried, and we both apologized once again for what Christee called the *nonsensical* Christee and then we laughed.

Christee had a way with words. Just like she could write songs, she could give people nicknames and come up with some idioms.

I asked Christee once why she had not sang for Nina's funeral service as she had sang when Raul and Tata (Dave's father) died, and she said, "My voice is not that good anymore. I have not practiced my voice exercises." And I believed it.

I told her she needed to practice and always be ready. What if I died? I wanted her to sing for me the song she had sang when she was in the church choir with Ms. Hollis. And she said, "You mean 'Gentlewoman.'" She laughed and said, "Okay, Mom, I'll sing for your funeral."

I remember how happy I was just to know she would sing for me at my funeral, and I told her how proud I was of her when she had sang for me at my law school graduation, and she said, "I was so proud of you, Mom. You are the 'wind beneath my wings,'" referring to the song she had sang for me.

Thinking back, she had not been singing in the mornings anymore.

Dear God, in my busy life, trying to help everyone around me, I was neglecting my own children and specially Christee who had this awful disease. "Dormant," the doctor would say, and I believed him too.

God, were you there?

Did you know what was going on with Christee?

What did You do?

Chapter 39

Twenty-Fifth Wedding Anniversary

Dave and I had wanted to have an anniversary party, but with Mom's recent death, we decided not to and instead go on a trip with Christee and Davey, just the family, and enjoy each other.

The eighteen summers and Christmas vacations, someone had told me once, should be enjoyed as the children will not follow you anymore after they are eighteen.

We found that was true to an extent. They wanted to go, but they had a schedule and calendar of their own. They had jobs, and they were in college. Davey said no, he couldn't go, and Christee said she would go for a few days with us but only if Ramon could come too. "He is part of the family, you know," and yes, he was, and it was the only way she would go with us. And just like before, when she wanted something, she negotiated it.

She wanted to go parasailing, rent a WaveRunner, and go snorkeling, and she didn't want to hear me tell her, "No, that's dangerous" or "No, you may get sick" or "It's too cold. Put a sweater and gloves on." I needed her with me, her smile and song, so I agreed to all she wanted.

On April 2005, in Los Cabos, Christee, Ramon, Dave, and I—what a nice family vacation. Although we missed Davey, we had all promised to enjoy the time together.

Of course, when we got there and I saw the prices of each and every item she wanted to do, I panicked. I didn't have that kind of money to spend on the trip, yet I wanted her and Ramon to have fun, but I didn't want to go into debt either.

Have you ever heard of timeshare presentations? I found out through the hotel that I could go to timeshare presentations, and they would give me vouchers to all the things Christee wanted to do without costing me any money. David was upset and said, "Just put it on a credit card." I said, "No, we are all going, and they start at seven thirty in the morning."

I had talked the people into giving me all the vouchers up front as Christee and Ramon would only be there for three days and Dave and I for six days, and they did. Christee and Ramon had fun and so did Dave and I, going to the sales presentations and challenging the sales people. It was only one hour a day.

The lady from the hotel later thanked me for booking all those presentations and even gave Dave and I discounts on activities we wanted. It turned out it was her first week on the job, and she had not done well in booking until we showed up.

Poor Ramon, I felt bad for him. Christee wanted to do all these outrageous activities, and he went along with her. At times, it appeared he did not enjoy some of them like parasailing, but he did, and Dave and I watched her being happy. The weather was beautiful, and she was warm and there was no cough, purple hands, or pain.

I particularly remember one afternoon when we all walked through the city. We had ventured out of the downtown and tourist area into the residential area, just walking. Ramon was holding Christee's hand and walking in front of Dave and me.

Ramon turned to Christee and said, "Look, see that building? We can come and live here, and you can have your veterinary shop here. Look at all the dogs. You would have plenty of customers." We all laughed and looked around; there were plenty of dogs walking by or just lazily lying down.

Those are the memories that hold me together, and I treasure them.

I pray, dear God, you don't ever let me forget those memories of my Christee and Ramon.

Not all memories are happy, but I treasure them too. The hotel had two pools, and it was next to the beach. We had agreed that in order for Mom not to be upset, Christee would swim in one pool and Mom in the other, and while we were together, Christee would use a T-shirt or whatever so that I would not have to see her back.

She had gone and tattooed her back during the blessed year of rebellion or the *nonsensical* Christee. It was such a disappointment to me and the cause of so many arguments with Christee. She was so petite, 5'1" and from ninety-five to 105 pounds, and her back so small, and she had gone and tattooed an angel the size of her entire back!

She told me once that she figured out that I would not be upset because she said that it was an angel, and since I loved angels, I would be okay with it. She was wrong. I was very upset—angel or not—and worried. Would the tattoo ink affect her lupus in any way?

At night, Dave took them to a night club while I relaxed, read, and prayed.

I think back on this vacation, and my heart warms up. And if I close my eyes, I can see her walking on the sand alongside Ramon, with her big smile, and I can almost hear her singing.

Christee would later tell us, "We are going to be so happy together. We all get along so good. Mom, Dad loves Ramon, and they can play the guitar together. We are going to be so happy, you'll see." She was happy at that moment and so was I!

Chapter 40

A Silly Cough

The summer of 2005, we lost my mother-in-law, Elsie. Once again, there was sadness in our family, and Dave and I reflected that God had given us so much earlier in our lives, and now, He had begun to take away our loved ones, but we understood they were all getting older, and we expected that.

Don't you? Aren't we all supposed to bury our parents, the older generation?

Christee had developed a cough. It was like when one has a dry throat, not continuous, but occasional, and at times, it was annoying. I remember telling Christee to please call the doctor about the cough. She said she would.

Then the cough sort of developed into a little giggle. You heard the tiny cough, turned to see Christee, and you would see a smile, and she would say, "The doctor says it's the medicine he has given me." That was meant for you to shut up. She didn't want to hear any comments.

One day, I heard a commercial about a cough institute in Los Angeles, and I told Christee about it, and she said she would call the insurance and ask her doctor about it. She still liked her doctor and was not about to change.

Then the cough was no more. Her friend had given her some of her asthma medicine, and it had helped with the cough. I was upset about it. She needed to change doctors. Why hadn't he given her that medicine before? Dave and I paid plenty of money for her insurance, and she was having someone give her medicine because the doctor was not prescribing it.

I was no longer happy, and I was now pushing Christee again to take care of herself and to push the doctor and ask for a breathing test and whatever other things he needed to do to make sure she was okay. And she said, "Mom, he did the breathing test, and he said my lungs are okay."

Christee was writing again a new song she wrote for Ramon. Well, the truth of the matter is that I don't know if it was for him or about him. I imagined she did after I heard the lyrics. This was not a heart-wrenching, sad, everyone-dead type of song; it was a heartwarming and moving song but still had some melancholy to it.

Almost as if she knew what was happening.

Christee could play the guitar, but if it was cold, her fingers would get purple, so Ramon began to play guitar for her and accompanied her in her singing. I was sad she wasn't playing her guitar. We had bought the guitar for her after she had won the songwriting contest.

I was happy to see Ramon and Christee together. They had so much in common, and you could see their happiness. She wanted to cook for Ramon and began to learn to cook from Dave. She would often make fun of me, saying, "I can't believe, Mom, you don't know how to cook yet."

One day, she asked if I could get up early and cook chorizo and eggs for her and Ramon; his grandma had given us some kind of special chorizo, and I agreed to but reminded her they would have to eat it regardless of the taste, and she laughed. "I don't think you can screw that up, Mom."

At breakfast, she began to make funny faces and started putting her fingers in her mouth. She pulled a piece of clear wrap, and then they all laughed. She could barely speak, and she accused me of trying to kill them. I had forgotten to take the clear wrapper off the chorizo. And we all laughed.

She laughed and said, "Stick to character pancakes, Mom. Those are good." Ever since they were little, I would make pancakes for them, and the shapes were so odd, never round. I would tell them they were different characters, and I would make up things like "That's a hippo or an elephant or a pot." I also put fruit in the pancakes, and they loved them.

I still make the pancakes for Davey, and he seems to enjoy them, but we don't talk much about the shapes anymore.

The giggle of a cough was still there, and fall and winter would be coming soon, and I was worried she would get worse.

Chapter 41

She Finally Agreed—A New Doctor!

Early 2006, I invited Christee to go with me to Europe, but she once again said no. Her studies were first, she was about to finish her BA, and all of a sudden, she was in a hurry to graduate. She was looking and thinking of the University of New Mexico. They had a good veterinary program.

Dave and I began to discuss the possibility of buying an investment home in Arizona for her to have something after vet school if she wanted to "set up shop." She liked the idea very much, not that she would live in Arizona, but that was where we could afford to buy.

Before I left for Europe in April, I told her that by the time I came back, I wanted her to have a new doctor. This was no longer a request. I reminded her that Ramon deserved and probably wanted a healthy girlfriend. She agreed; her friend gave her the name of her doctor, and she called the insurance to make the change.

Thank God, she finally realized that she needed to change doctors. She was doing better with the medicine her friend gave her, and the doctor had refused to give her a prescription for it.

While I was in Europe, Christee conference called (Skype) me. She was excited and smiling. Dave had taken her to Arizona, and they were looking for houses. I reminded both to look for "fixer-uppers only, and asked 'what about the new doctor?'"

Chapter 42

A Phone Call and My Heart Sunk

Dave and I were coming back from Vegas when we got a phone call from Christee. "Mom, how far are you?" My heart began to throb, and I spoke with a calm voice so as not to scare her or not to show my worry. "By Barstow, Christee," I replied and closed my eyes; I was afraid of what was coming next.

"Oh," she said, "then I better tell you now so you won't be so angry when you get here." *Christee, are you okay? Where are you?*

What? A new dog! "No." I remember telling her that she, Ramon, the dogs, and the bird (Ramon's bird) would have to find a place to stay. I did not want my house to continue being a zoo. She didn't even listen to a word I said. "You will love her. She is so tiny and cute, Mom, and I named her Twinkee Lee, and, Mom . . . Scoobiedoobi needed a pet. He is so happy!"

Scoobiedoobi, or Zono as I call him, is a Labrador mix that she had brought back with her as a reminder of the *nonsensical* Christee year, and we had Dustee Rose too. The last thing I wanted was another dog.

But I could breathe with a sense of relief. She was okay, not sick, which was always my fear, but this time, her voice didn't have the energy or enthusiasm as always. I knew something was wrong.

Summer of 2006
Christee Lee; Scoobiedoobi (Zono), a black Labrador mix;
Dustee Rose, a tan, terrier and whippet mix; and Twinkee
Lee, a mini doxie dachshund.

She had called the insurance only to find out they had made a mistake
and the change would not be effective until the following month. That
was no longer acceptable to me, and I called them and demanded the
change immediately. The next day, we were able to make a doctor's
appointment. Of course, it wasn't until a few weeks later, but at least
she had a new doctor, and she agreed that I could go with her to meet
the new doctor.

I think it was mid-June 2006. Ramon and Christee went shopping.
Dave and I were in the kitchen when they came back. She had a beaming
smile, bigger than usual, and we were all standing around the kitchen
island as she said, "You like my ring, Mom?" and she extended her arm
toward me and her tiny hand to reveal a beautiful ring. Ramon had his
arm around her shoulder and sported a big smile too. I can close my

eyes and see them, both with an awe-inspiring smile and an aura of enchantment around them; I knew they were in love.

I remember saying, "What a beautiful friendship ring," teasingly, and with her good nature and humor, she replied, "No, Mom, it's an engagement ring." We all hugged. I looked at her, and she said, "Don't worry, I'll finish school first." Although I knew this day would come and I was truly happy, in the back of my mind, I couldn't help but worry. How would this illness affect her marriage? But I was happy. She had finally found the "right guy" she had been looking for.

The next few weeks were blissful, talking about the type of wedding she wanted and if Dad and I would be footing the bill. It was fun talking about a wedding that she promised wouldn't happen until after graduation. Although, I hadn't asked if she was talking about the upcoming graduation or after the graduate (vet school) work. But I didn't want to spoil it, and I did not ask her.

I remember telling her that my family's tradition was that "Mom and Dad would buy the wedding dress only." She smiled and said, "Mom, it won't be expensive. You'll see, only family and close friends." In my heart I knew we would do whatever she wanted, and this time, I would negotiate better to have my friends there too.

Chapter 43

Reserving a Priest and Church

It was a happy time. Was my guard down again?

Oh dear God, it almost seems that I am in the midst of a fog. Nothing is clear . . . My timelines run into each other. Everything happened so fast.

Not sure anymore what month it was. We had an event at St. Matthias Church, and after Mass, Christee approached Father Gorman, the priest that had married David and I and had blessed her on the day she came home from the hospital after being born and also baptized her, and asked him, "Father Gorman, when I get married, will you be the priest, and can I get married at this church?" We no longer lived there, and it was not our parish.

These memories bring tears to my eyes and pain to my heart, but I rejoice in God that I have these memories to treasure and remind me that she was happy and alive.

Father Gorman said, "Sure," with his Irish accent and said, "When is this wedding happening, Christee?" With her cutest face and smile she said, "As soon as I finish with school. About five years, Father." Father Gorman laughed and said, "Christee, I am too old. You are going to have to come every day to Huntington Park and give me vitamins to keep me alive for five more years." And Christee smiled and said, "Will you, Father?" And he replied, "Yes, Christee, if I am alive."

Father Gorman is still alive, and when I see him, I can only think of that conversation. *I am happy to see him. He hugs me and blesses*

Dave and me almost as a routine, but something inside me tells me he is thinking of Christee's wedding. The one he never got to officiate.

Time is moving fast in my head. So fast, I just don't know anymore what happened first. I pause and pray.

Dear Lord, help me put this in writing as I don't want to forget. As painful as it is, I don't want to forget not even one word or a moment of these summer days.

Chapter 44

A New Doctor

The new doctor was nice. It was a modest office, not like the "other doctor." There were hardly any patients there, and I was apprehensive, thinking if this doctor was any good. *Where are the patients?* I thought. *Or was he so good that he did not like his patients to wait?* He came out to the reception area and called us in; he was informal and had a nice demeanor and a pleasant smile.

He asked questions about Christee and told us he had not yet received the records from the other facility. I was not surprised; they were always so busy. Christee coughed or giggled a few times, and he said, "I don't like that cough," and he listened to her chest and lungs and asked Christee when was the last time she had x-rays done. Christee could not remember if it was two years or more. He issued a request for x-rays "stat."

We really liked this doctor. He wanted to update all labs and exams and did not like the cough Christee had. He also expressed the fact that he did not attribute the cough to asthma. "It just doesn't sound like an asthmatic cough."

I went with Christee to the x-rays from there. They said they would send them to the doctor, and he would call us for the results. We had a new appointment already to review them. Christee commented, "I should have changed doctors sooner." I said nothing.

On July 31, 2006, we went in to review the x-rays findings. There was only one patient waiting. The doctor came out to the reception area again and called us in, but this time, he did not have a smile, and he took us into his office, not an examining room. It was too fast for me; I didn't even have a chance to react or think about it.

He looked at Christee and said, "The problem is not asthma. I need you to see a pulmonologist right away." I remember Christee turning to face me with a questioning expression. I asked the doctor what was wrong. "Not sure. I need you to see a pulmonologist. I already arranged for you to see one. He is expecting you, go." And he ushered us out of his office.

The nurse handed me the consultation request and the address to the pulmonologist and told us more or less where the office was located. We had the x-rays on hand. We got in the car and neither one of us spoke.

We got to the doctor's office. There were several people waiting, but the receptionist asked for the x-rays and took them to the back. The doctor wanted to see them. She came back and told us the doctor needed Christee to have a different type or angle of x-ray. I'm not sure anymore of what exactly she said. She gave us the order and sent us to an office downstairs. What was going on? Why didn't the doctor tell me what he suspected? I didn't say anything. I was scared, and I didn't want to frighten Christee.

After Christee had the x-rays, the technician said he would send them upstairs and for us to go and wait. When we got there, the receptionist told us to wait; they would send the x-rays upstairs, and the doctor would see us.

Christee and I sat there in the waiting room; neither one of us was talking.

The nurse called out Christee's name, and we both got up and looked at each other. She smiled, and she walked in front of me. The nurse took us to an examining room, and Christee sat at the examining table. I sat down in a chair across from the table; we were still not talking.

The doctor walked in, shook hands with Christee and then with me. He had the x-rays on hand. He turned to face me and said, "How long has Christee had this cough?" and before I answered, Christee said,

"About two years, it started—" but he cut her off, and he looked at me and said, "How could you have ignored her cough?" His voice was so accusatory and with disdain. I think he caught us off guard, and I didn't know what to say.

Almost immediately Christee spoke, and her voice sounded angry but with poise, which commanded respect. "Don't talk to her like that. Look at me. I am an adult."

The doctor turned to see her and said, "How old are you?" She said, "I am twenty-two years old." And immediately she said, "What is wrong with me? What do the x-rays show?"

The doctor turned to look at me and then at her and said, "You have scleroderma. It's a—" And then I heard Christee say, "No, God, not that." Her voice had anguish to it and was loud with disbelief. I had never heard that word, and I asked the doctor, "What is that?" and turned to look at Christee. Before the doctor answered me, Christee said, "I saw on TV a program of a woman that had that illness. It was awful."

The doctor said, "It's scarring and thickening of the lungs. Her lungs are almost gone. I am surprised she can breathe on her own. She needs to see a specialist. Take her immediately to UCLA or USC. Do it today, now!"

Christee got off the table and walked to me and, with a tender voice, said, "Mom, get up. Let's go." She turned to thank the doctor, and he said, "I am sorry." I got up, looked at Christee, and she had a half smile and said, "You shouldn't be talking to Mom like that." And she pulled me out the door.

She held my hand all the way down the corridor, to the elevator, and to the parking lot. She asked if I wanted her to drive, and I said no. I drove to my office and neither one of us spoke.

Chapter 45

Where Do We Go from Here?

I told Christee I was very hungry and for her to go and get us something to eat. I don't remember now what I told her I wanted and from where. I just wanted her out of the office as I needed to make some urgent calls. I knew she was tired, and the last thing she wanted to do was to go out and buy food, but she took the car keys and left. I think she needed the time alone too.

I called the health insurance customer service and explained to them what the pulmonologist had told me to get her to UCLA or USC immediately. The young man began by telling me, "The hospital that you belong to is—" and I stopped him. I didn't care to hear what hospital we belonged or was closer. I said I wanted an approval to both hospitals and now.

I was relieved to find out that both hospitals were available through our insurance, and they asked me which one I wanted. Oh dear God, I had no clue as I knew nothing about the doctors they had and the programs they had for this disease. I asked the young man to give me two names of rheumatologists at both hospitals, and I would pick one and then call them back.

I had the names and now what?

The website for UCLA revealed that they did have a research program for scleroderma, and it was headed by a woman, Dr. Grossman. When I called, I found out that she was not taking any more patients. I explained to the young lady that had answered the phone the urgency of the problem, and she was nice and promised to give the doctor the message. But inside me I knew there would be no callback. "She is not taking new patients" had been her answer.

I remembered an acquaintance of mine. I had heard once someone said her ex-husband was a doctor at UCLA. I called several people to obtain her number. I explained the situation and asked if she would give me his name and number. Perhaps he knew the doctors at UCLA and could urge the doctor to accept Christee. She was so sweet. She acknowledged she had not spoken to him for years and that he had just moved to New York but would get the phone number from their daughter.

The phone rang, and it was a woman calling from New York. She identified herself as a nurse and had the information for a doctor at UCLA. She also said, "Call her now. She is waiting for your call." I hope and pray that, in my haste to hang up and call UCLA, I had thanked her. I had failed to get her number and name.

When I called the number she had given me, it was a doctor's office. I immediately identified myself and the young lady said, "Oh yes, Doctor is waiting for your call." The doctor answered the phone. She was nice and soft spoken. She asked me several questions about Christee's condition and asked if I had all of Christee's records, and I said yes. She asked me to hold, and when she came back to the phone, she said, "I spoke to Dr. Grossman. She has agreed to see Christee. No promises of any type other than to see her for a consultation. Here is the number. Call her nurse, and they will schedule you right away."

Dr. Grossman's office gave me an appointment for August 3, 2006. The nurse cautioned that Christee and all records including x-rays needed to be brought at the time of the appointment. I hung up, and Christee got there.

Christee was upset. The traffic was bad, she forgot what I wanted, and she wasn't hungry and wanted to know if we could just go home and eat there. I said, "Yes, that's a good idea." And we went home.

Chapter 46

What the Records Revealed

When we got home, I called Christee's previous doctor. Yes, Dr.—. It pains me so much to mention his name. I had trusted him; Christee had put all her trust and faith in his knowledge and care for his patients, and he had let her down. He, of course, didn't know what was going on, and I didn't need him to know at that moment.

I needed all of Christee's records, and I needed them fast. He, of course, was busy and could not take my call. I insisted to speak to the administrator and told her of the need of the records as we were seeing a new doctor, and she would not see Christee without the records. I reminded her of all the years Christee was a patient and that she should ask Dr.—for his approval and the urgency.

I offered to pay extra for the copying and she agreed. Greed, I knew they would accept. They always had patients waiting and waiting, always overbooking. Why didn't I see that before? He betrayed my Christee.

On August 3, 2006, we arrived at UCLA—Dave, Christee, Ramon, and I. Christee had spoken to Ramon, and he wanted to be there.

Dr. Grossman was pleasant and soft spoken and directed all her attention to Christee. She had asked Christee if she wanted all of us there or to be alone. Christee wanted all of us there. "In case I don't understand something, Mom always has questions," she had told the doctor. I was so afraid that I wasn't sure I could come up with any questions, but Christee was counting on me; I needed to be strong.

The doctor looked at the x-rays and commented that the scleroderma was very advanced. "How amazing that you are breathing without oxygen, Christee." I pointed to the records where I had discovered, while reviewing them, that in one of the breathing tests a year earlier, a technician had noted scleroderma on the findings and then again earlier in the year. Yet her doctor had never mentioned anything to her or even noted it in his notes.

She explained there was no cure for scleroderma, and the research was in its infancy as it is a very rare lung disease. I wanted to cry and hold Christee tightly against my chest and reassure her it was going to be all right. I needed to be strong. This was not the place to fall apart, not in front of her. Ramon was there, touching her shoulder, and she looked at him with a half smile and a twinkle in her eyes.

Dr. Grossman wanted to hospitalize Christee as soon as possible and put a team of doctors to examine and monitor her. She would immediately request a team if we accepted and Christee said yes, and then, as an afterthought, Christee asked, "What about school? I have finals next week." She was in such a hurry to finish school that she had enrolled in a summer class at Cerritos College.

Dr. Grossman told her not to worry about school or anything else. She would give her a note for the teacher, but Christee said no. She didn't want a note. She just wanted to finish. "Is it okay if I go to school?" And Dr. Grossman said, "Yes, but you must be ready for my phone call, and even if there are finals, you must get to the hospital within two hours after my call, or we lose the bed. Do you understand the importance of these?" And Christee said yes.

We all went home. David was at summer break, but I needed to make arrangements at work in order to be ready at moment's notice. The soonest the call would come was Monday, August 7, doctor had told us.

David and I had agreed that perhaps it was better if Christee kept going to school; at least her mind would be busy for a couple of hours with school.

I still wasn't sure what scleroderma was despite the doctor explaining it to us and giving us pamphlets to read. Christee had told her about her knowing what it was and described the episode of the documentary she had seen on one of those medical shows.

It was horrible to hear Christee describe the illness and crippling effects it had; I was shaken. Before we had gone upstairs to see Dr. Grossman at the hospital, I had gone to the bathroom and seen a young woman there, perhaps Christee's age, with some physical disabilities. Now I could see those characteristics in her as Christee was describing them.

I don't remember praying. I don't remember questioning God. My mind was blank, and it hurt—it hurt to even think of what this disease would do to my little girl.

Chapter 47

Weekend Plans

The next morning, I realized that we had weekend plans with my family in San Diego, and I told Dave we needed to cancel everything, and he agreed. But Christee was in the other room and heard our conversation and said, "Why are you canceling the plans?" I told her I was not in the mood to go, but she said, "Mom, go. You promised to take everyone to San Diego." I told her, "No, we are not going."

Her voice had this sharp and crisp tone to it, not angry but with determination when she said, "I have plans for the weekend too, Mom. I am not going to stay home and cry. I am going to go and have fun, and you and Dad should do the same." Then her tone softened and said, "Mom, if you don't go, they are going to ask why, and I don't want anyone to know anything now. Please go."

We went to San Diego, and she called me several times throughout the weekend just to say hello. She asked about the weather and how everyone was enjoying the weekend and told me about taking Twinkee to a dog's birthday party and how she had enjoyed it and that "Twinkee was the cutest of all the puppies."

How mature and grown up she was. She was thinking about us and not her. She wanted to reassure me that she was doing fine and not to worry about her. She didn't have self-pity and didn't want any from anyone.

Chapter 48

Oxygen and Food

On Tuesday, August 8, 2012, the call came in about twelve thirty in the afternoon. A bed was available, and we needed to go to UCLA and admit Christee right away. Christee was in school, and I was in Glendale. I told them we would be there right away.

The traffic was bad in the 405 Freeway. I guess it was always bad, but on that day, it was worse. We needed to be there by a certain time, and I was worried we would lose the bed. I called the doctor several times and let her know about the traffic, and she said she would let them know. We were not talking much, but out of nowhere, Christee said, "No wonder I couldn't sing anymore. It hurt so much, and I couldn't reach the notes. Mom, the doctor never saw the results from the breathing test, and he just kept telling me it was asthma and that the lupus was dormant. *Que doctorcito* (What a doctor)." She did not sound angry, and her tone of voice had no rancor to it.

Christee was admitted, and Dr. Grossman and her team came up to see her the next morning. There were six or seven doctors: there was a heart specialist, rheumatoid arthritis specialist, gastrointestinal specialist, pulmonologist, internist, and a couple of student doctors doing their residency. They were all very pleasant and their bedside manners were excellent, and above all, they spoke to her with respect and dignity.

They all directed their questions to Christee. She had said at one point, "Thank you so very much that you all agreed to see me." In the midst of it all, her good manners were there, and she remembered to thank everyone. I was proud of her strength and courage and composure and SMILE.

They immediately put her on oxygen and on a battery of medicines for her stomach pain; it turned out it was not heartburn but something else (I don't remember the name) and needed more than the antiacid medicine she had been taking.

Christee was funny and liked to joke with us but normally not with strangers. She was shy, but I remember listening to her tell the doctors, "Ah, you want me to be able to breathe and eat too." And with that, I knew how nervous and scared she was but was trying to make light of everything to make everyone around her feel comfortable and that everything was all right.

With the oxygen and new medicines, Christee immediately began to feel good and began to ask for food and actually eat it. It reminded me of when she was little and had been hospitalized and the nurses were amazed at such a small child asking for steak and broccoli soup and eating everything they gave her. It was the same now, but what they were giving her was not enough, and I would make the extra trips to the hospital cafeteria.

"Mom, I can eat and my stomach doesn't hurt. I can walk to the bathroom without stopping to rest and catch my breath. Mom, *Diosito* (God) is going to make me okay. Ah, Mom." And I looked at her and smiled and said, "Of course, He will. You are in the best hospital and with the best doctors." She held my hand and smiled at me. Neither one of us cried, but there was a shimmer in our eyes as we both held off our tears.

Christee received an e-mail from her teacher saying he would not excuse her from taking the exam and she would fail the class if the exam was not taken timely. Christee had notified him of the impending hospitalization, but her teacher had said, "There is nothing wrong with you. I don't see that you are sick." I had been angry when she told me that, but Christee was stubborn and didn't want anyone to know of her illness. She would rather have them believe she was okay.

She asked the nurses if they would allow her to use one of their offices to plug in her computer and take the test as the teacher had agreed that she could take the test one day early over the Internet. They agreed but tried to discourage her from taking the test. The doctors were upset too when the nurses told them and asked Christee for the e-mail or phone to call him, but Christee said no. She took the test and was upset when she didn't get an A. "I should have studied more," she said.

Dear God, was she so focused on her present not to think of the uncertain future?

I began to get upset and short-tempered with people and she noticed. She was watching me, and one day, she said, "Mom, don't do that, please . . ." and she began to cry. I looked at her and said, "What is wrong? I am not doing anything, and I didn't snap at anyone either. Please don't cry." I truly didn't know why she was crying.

I went to hold her and console her, and she said, "You have never eaten any leftovers from our plates, not even when we were little. You don't like for people to touch your plate or your food, and now, you are eating my leftovers." And now she was uncontrollably crying, and so was I.

We had found a stupid and silly reason for us to cry, to relieve the tension that we had both held for so long in the hope of being strong for each other.

I told her I wasn't eating her leftovers. I was being lazy and didn't want to walk to the cafeteria. I told her how silly I had been all those years, getting angry when they, Davey or her, picked something from my plate and, in my anger, not eating anymore from that plate but serving myself another plate. I told her that I loved her so much that I would eat whatever they told me if it would make her healthy, and we hugged and cried until the nurse came in. Another test was waiting for Christee.

One morning, when she woke up, she got up and went to the rest room. I hadn't heard any noise, and I didn't wake up. I was tired, and I guess sleeping on a chair was taking its toll. She had urged me before to go home at night and that she would be all right, but I had told her I would not leave her alone.

After the doctors came, made their round, and told us what they would do the next day, then I would go home to shower and change and then come back. Dave or Ramon would be there by then.

But that morning, I was tired, and I did not hear her get up. The doctors came in and woke me up and asked about Christee. I got up and went to look for her in the restroom, and she was not there. They called the nurse, and she didn't know either, and they were upset that she was not in bed. They paged Christee, and she answered from the cafeteria. She was hungry and didn't want to wake me up.

Chapter 49

Promises

The doctors were furious at Christee for walking around by herself, and one of them reminded her how sick she was. "You can go into cardiac arrest. Your lungs are very damaged. You must take it easy." And she said, "But this is the best I've felt in a long, long time." They made her lie down in bed and told her she needed to call someone even to go to the restroom. She was visibly upset. They checked her, and they left.

"Mom."

"Yes, Christee," I replied.

"Promise me something. Please promise me."

"Yes, Christee, anything you want."

"If I get really sick, please make sure my hair is combed, my face is clean, no spit on the side of my mouth, and put some makeup on me. Please make me look good. Please put a ribbon on my hair like you did when I was little. Please, Mom."

"Yes, Christee, I promise." There were no tears on her eyes, but her voice was quivering, and she was full of resolve.

"Mom . . . what the doctor did was wrong, don't you think?"

"What doctor, Christee?"

"You know, he didn't even check the results from the lab. My breathing tests just went into the file, and when I went to see him, he just said everything is okay but never saw the results, Mom. Mom, do something about it. Please, so it won't happen to anyone else. We could have been here a year ago, don't you think, Mom?

I remember just telling her, "Don't think about that. Let's concentrate on you health right now."

"Promise me you'll do something, Mom, so it won't happen to anyone else. He should have seen those results and told me about them."

"Yes, Christee, I promise you, but not right now."

"Thank you, Mom." And she went back to the book she was reading.

It was early Sunday morning, and we were still at the hospital. A Eucharistic minister came and offered us Communion. Christee asked her if she would come back later. She wanted Ramon, her, and I to take Communion together, and he was not there yet but would be coming later.

Neither Christee nor I thought of the inconvenience to the lady. After all, they were volunteers, and they had a family too. She was so polite and kind and immediately agreed to come back later.

I had called David to bring me some ribbon for Christee's hair. I had washed her hair, and she wanted a pink ribbon. We had laughed after I had asked David to bring the ribbon. Christee had commented that I should go downstairs to the gift shop to buy it. "Mom, you know he is going to forget. You are going to be upset and go downstairs to buy it. Why ask him for it?" She was right: he would forget it.

We talked about all kinds of things, and out of nowhere, she brought up the nonsensical Christee year. I told her not to think on any negative in her life and that we were going to concentrate on all the good and positive, but she said, "You made me strong and responsible. I am sorry for what I put you through." we hugged and kissed, and before the tears began, we were interrupted.

David and Ramon got to the hospital room, and Dave pulled out of his pocket a pink piece of yarn, and we all laughed. He had forgotten the ribbon, and at the gift shop, they didn't have any for him to buy, so they sent him to the flower shop. They were kind enough to give him a piece of yarn. Christee thanked him and then asked me to put it on her hair. It wasn't long enough to braid. It looked silly on her head, but she was happy.

We all prayed together, and when the Eucharistic minister came back, Ramon, Christee, and I took Communion.

Chapter 50

A Young Lady Making BIG Decisions

I don't remember how many of the doctors from the team came in, but they wanted to discuss something with Christee, and she said it was okay for all of us to be there.

The team had decided, after all the tests she had undergone, that they wanted to give her a dose of chemotherapy to see if it would slow down the growth of the scleroderma. They didn't know if it would work or not. "It is experimental."

Christee needed to decide immediately as they wanted to give it to her that night to observe her and then she would be released Monday or Tuesday, depending how it went. Christee had questions regarding her fertility issues, and they said to call Dr. Grossman and discuss it with her. They would leave the order with the nurses pending Christee's decision.

"Mom, can they harvest my eggs and save them?"

I called Dr. Grossman who was kind and who listened to what I had to say and then replied, "We are talking about saving Christee's life. There is no time for harvesting eggs, and she may never be able to have children regardless. You need to convince her that is all that we can do now."

There were family and friends visiting Christee when I got back to the room, and we needed to make a decision. Ramon went out the room to talk to me and commented that he thought she should do it and asked what I thought. I remember we had a long conversation about his love for her and not caring if they ever had children. He wanted her alive and well. We were all broken, but we all wanted her healthy and, above all, alive.

Christee had a member of the family go find me and Ramon and, when we went in, just said, "Did she say yes or no, Mom?"

I replied, "No time."

"Mom, tell the nurses to go ahead. Let them know to give me the 'thing.' Mom, you are going to have to work harder to buy me some wigs," and then she smiled.

Chapter 51

A Surge of Energy and a Song

I don't remember what day we came back from the hospital, Monday or Tuesday, but Christee was full of energy and had missed one or two of her friends' birthdays and was mortified and wanted to go and visit them . . . and I said NO. She needed to be in bed and rest. The doctors had told her so.

She had been sent home with an oxygen tank, and I was worried too that she would run out. They would not deliver the supply of oxygen home until the next day. "Mom, please don't hold me back. I am alive and I feel good. Please let me go. I don't want to argue with you." Ramon came home that evening, and they stayed home. Her friends would come and visit during the week.

The next day, I made breakfast for her and told her I would go to the office for a couple of hours and then be back before lunch. We had made menu cards, like at the hospital, and she would pick whatever she felt like eating, and I would make it. Of course, nothing complicated: oatmeal, eggs, salads, chicken—those sort of things. We had had so much fun making the menus on the computer and then printing a whole bunch of sheets. She would fax me the menu at the office, and then I could stop and buy whatever it was I needed for her lunch.

When I came home, Christee had cleaned the den and her bedroom, "Don't tell me anything. I have a lot of energy and feel real good. I did everything little by little, not to get tired. Believe me, Mom, I did not strain myself at all . . . I wanted to help out a little bit."

All week, she cleaned the house a little at a time. She had also washed her clothes, towels, and linen, and I was worried that she was overdoing it. It had not been discussed but sort of implied that she would not go to school in September, and that was a relief.

Christee's birthday was coming up, August 22, and she wanted to go and have her hair colored and highlighted, and I said, "No, not until we ask the doctor." We had a doctor's appointment coming on the eighteenth, and Christee was laughing and making fun of me. "They have me on chemotherapy, and you are worried about bleach on my hair?" She wanted to take a bath, and I wouldn't let her, and she laughed. "Right, hot water, it might hurt me."

We went to the doctor's appointment, and I told her about Christee's surge of energy and that I was worried. After the exams, the doctor expressed concern that perhaps not enough chemotherapy had been applied, and another round may be needed. She addressed all of Christee's "wants" and approved of them and told me, "It's okay for her to do things. So long as she does not strain herself, let her." Another appointment was set, and we left.

When we got in the car, she and Ramon sat in the back, and she said she wanted the four of us to go out to eat. She wanted to go to the Cerritos Mall. On the way to the mall, she took off her oxygen mask, and she began singing a song and asked Dave, "Dad, do you know the name of the song?" Dave replied that he had heard of it but did not remember the name. She then said with a sweet and tender voice, "I want to sing that song when I get married. I'll sing that song as I am walking down the aisle toward Ramon. Just like you sang to Mom when you two got married while she was walking down the aisle."

I held my tears back, and I turned slightly to look at Dave, who was also close to tears, and then she continued singing the song. We do not remember what the song was or the lyrics to look for it. We never asked Ramon. Perhaps he knows what song it is. Perhaps it is best left alone.

Dave and I have spoken about that day many times, and we have both thanked God that He allowed us to hear her singing one more time. She was happy, full of joy and in love. If she was afraid of the uncertain future, she was certainly not letting us in on it. She wanted us to share in her present, and her present was blissful and with song in mind.

Chapter 52

Twenty-Third Birthday

She reminded me that her birthday was on Tuesday, and she wanted to have a party. I had told her no parties. She needed to rest. She had complained her legs hurt some, and I had attributed it to the walk to the doctors and the visit to the mall although we did not let her walk that much.

On Monday, she told me she had invited people to the house for her birthday the next day, and all I needed to do was to order food. "Mom, please. I want to celebrate my birthday. Please, I feel good, and I want them to see me feeling good. Not when I am sick and I begin to lose my hair with that chemotherapy. Mom, I know you are tired, but the house is clean, and you don't have to do anything. Just order the food, and Ramon or Davey will pick it up, please." She had planned her own birthday party, had cleaned the house, and was looking forward to seeing family and friends.

She complained of having to carry the oxygen tank and then immediately thank God for it as she could "make it to the bathroom from the den without having to stop and rest in the living room."

"Christee, why didn't you tell me of this before?" I asked her, "Because you are just like Nina Mago. You worry about everything," she answered.

That afternoon, Christee and I sat at the dining table. She was on the computer doing something, and I was reading something. Dave came home from running an errand and sat at the table with us, and the three of us just sat there. No conversation, just enjoying each of us all quiet and in harmony. Ramon showed up after work and sat at the table too. Christee, who was closest to me, turned to me and commented, "Look at them, Mom." Dave and Ramon were talking about music. Ramon asked Dave, "Can I bring a guitar? And you show me how to play "My Girl." Christee looked at me, her face beaming with joy and pride, and there was such tenderness in her voice. "We are going to be so happy." And then out of nowhere, she said, "Thank you, Mom."

The next day, friends and family came to celebrate her birthday, and she was happy and had a smile despite the fact that she had noticed that morning that she was losing some hair. She hadn't told me about it. When I told her to fix her hair because it looked messy, she, with her witty laughter, responded, "It's okay like that so they won't notice that it's thinner. It started to fall off." And I couldn't say anything other than to go into my room and cry.

Where was she getting all the strength?

I hadn't picked up a prayer book for days nor could I recite the Lord's Prayer without stumbling on the words or having to go back and forth as I had no concentration for prayer or anything else.

Was it denial, anger—what was it? I don't know what it was, but on that day, I prayed again, and I thanked God that He allowed me to see my baby happy on her twenty-third birthday. I often think about that day.

What did she know, and how did she feel? She had insisted on celebrating her birthday with family and friends.

She got so many gifts: shoes, clothes, robes, and some beautiful earrings Ramon bought her, flowers and cookies. But she was most appreciative of everyone coming to see her. No sadness, no crying, just her usual happy self and making fun of her oxygen tank in tow.

At the end of the night, after everyone had left, she said, "Thank you, Mom, for letting me celebrate my birthday. Oh yeah, and paying for the food." She was always appreciative and loved to thank us and others.

Thank-You Letters:

TO: MOM & DADDY

DADDY:
I want to thank you so much for always being there for me. There are so many reasons why, but so little ways to return the thanks. I am sorry for disobeying you. You were not that stricked with me when I did things wrong that were not that bad, but when I real messed up you got on my case which was good. Thank you for always showing me new and exciting things. I remember once I was feeling low and sad, all you did was sat next to me, talked with me and then sung and played the guitar. Daddy even when I wasn't

Mommy

Daddy

low or even when I wasn't sad, when you played
me guitar and song to me, I just got so happy when
you were sick, losing you were and really couldn't sing so
good as you used to I still got happy when I heard your
sweet voice daddy thank you for everthing and for being
there when I needed you without you I wouldn't be able
to do half of the things that I do now daddy you have
shown me so much in the last 13 years. I also remember
when I was little I promised you I would stay (little) intel
well, sorry I feel I can't tell you enough times dad
I will always love you for ever and ever, Thank you!!!

Dawen

Spot

Aubtee

A   TR

©Jim Henson Productions, Inc.

MOM

Thank you so much for everything you have
done for me, and for being there. I know
sometimes we would get in fights and I am
sorry, I know you are right but sometimes people
will not admit they are wrong like me for instance.
Thank you for teaching me new things and helping
me write letters that needed to sound businessy
(business like). Also for typing a few - well ok, alot of
my reports, I realy needed the help. I want to
thank you for making me feel special and
for the advice you would give me when I really
needed the advice, Mom I Love you. I
know you think I don't trust
you, but I do, mom with my
life. mom thank you for sharing
your advice, your laughter, your
love and your friendship.

Love and
Dad
mom

you are a true mother and the best mother
in the world, thats the truth. I Love you.
I cant thank you enough MoM, I Love
you and will always love you and I will
never stop loving you. When we spght I
still love you ok. don't forget that.
thank you mom, and I do trust you.
P.s. mom thank you for coming in my
room tucking me in and kissing me
good night/P.s. Daddy Thank you for
reading the bible to me and Laura/
I really learned alot./P.P.S MoM
Thank you for putting up with
the girls and me at palm
Springs. I ♥ U both
Love ♥ Christee Lee Rivera

To: Mommee!!

Yeah!! Happy Birthday. To day is your day to shine!
Mom I want you to know that no matter what stupid
idiotic thing I do or say I LOVE You. Thank you for
being not only my mom but also my friend. You always
know how to make things better. You are a very very
smart lady and I hope that some day some how I end up
smart, caring, passionate, energetic, and motivated like
you.
Mom I can't take back all the hurt I put you through but I
want you to know that I honestly, and sincerely
apologize for those awful years I put you through. Mom
we don't know what dabree lies ahead on the road through
life, but together we can help each other and weave our
way around the troubles.
Thank you for never turning your back on me even
though at times it seemed like I turned my back on you.
THANK YOU!! That is the true definition of the Best
Mom in the WORLD!!!!!!!! I love you Mom Have a great
day and don't let anyone ruin it. (Not even me okay!!)

From: Christee Lee Rivera

Chapter 53

Raul Perez Memorial Scholarship Fund

I told you about my brother-in-law Raul having been diagnosed with stage-four gallbladder cancer on that May day back in 1996. We had, as a family, gathered together then too to pray and ask God for a miracle.

Would He listen like He did before when He allowed Mother to live those ten years and to truly enjoy life itself?

"Cure him, Lord. His children and wife need him," we would pray. Christee prayed too along with the family but would also sing. Christee often went to see him and even went with me to accompany him to try alternative medicines. There had been other cancer patients at that clinic too, and Christee sang "Here I Am, Lord" and "On Eagles' Wings," and Raul enjoyed her singing, and she was happy to see him smile and the other patients too.

Raul died on October 26, 1996. The pain was so intense, he was having problems seeing or talking because of the pain, and he had been asking the family to just let him go. He was tired of the agonizing pain.

Had God heard any of us?

After Raul's death, Christee was devastated. She loved him so much. But in the midst of the pain and anguish, she still managed to sing for his funeral at the grave site. She had been strong; Dave played the guitar for her. It was a cold and rainy morning on the day of his funeral. Her voice was strong and steady, and her hands had been rosy as there was not any sign of her illness then.

She sang beautifully and brought tears to many and received compliments from many too. She was thirteen years of age, and to hear the strength of her voice, to see her character, and experience the solemnity of the occasion in her singing made all of us proud, especially Dave and me.

My family never celebrated El Dia de los Muertos (The Day of the Dead), but Christee did celebrate it in high school and took all kinds of newspaper clippings celebrating and mentioning Raul's life accomplishments and his death. She wanted everyone to know about him; she was proud of the legacy he was leaving. All the schoolwork she had, yet she found time to pay homage to her uncle; it was touching to see her sensibility and her kind spirit.

She had been very sad and did not want to eat. Aside from Raul's illness and death, she had lost her dog a few months before, and her grief had compounded. I had put my foot down when her dog had died and told her, "NO more dogs." It was too much work for her. No one helped her with cleaning and feeding them, and her schoolwork was too much, and her day, too long. But her sadness was so grave that I was afraid she would get sick or go into depression, and that November 1996, I brought home Dustee Rose, the mixed terrier-whippet dog, which I mentioned earlier that had been my comfort on that horrible nonsensical Christee year.

And now, ten years later, I had finally set up a nonprofit memorial scholarship fund in Raul's name. Christee had helped me address and send out invitations to the upcoming First Dinner Dance event to be held on August 25, 2006. Now with Christee's diagnosis only a few days earlier on July 31, I didn't know what to do. My daughter . . . Oh God.

Christee was my first and only priority and the only thing in my mind. I prayed that everyone would understand.

I had procrastinated all those years thinking my sister and her children were not ready for the stress of participating in the nonprofit events, and now it might all have to be put on hold, and for how long?

I remember on those days waking up as if in a fog. The whole day never clearing up, and the heaviness of my heart was such that I could not sleep at all, and it all went on and on. I knew I could not follow through with the event. What would they say or do? It had been my idea, and now, I would be asking them to do it, putting it on their shoulders.

I discussed with the committee the fact that they would have to take over and oversee all the pending planning and events. The committee understood my child came first. I am not sure they knew exactly what was wrong or even the gravity of her illness. I myself could barely understand what was going on. The committee suggested everything should be cancelled until Christee was better.

I came home and told the family the event would be cancelled, but Christee wouldn't hear of it. She urged that I do not cancel the event. "Mom, it took you ten years to finally set it up. If you cancel it now, you will never do it again. Mom, please don't cancel."

She was pleading for something that was not for her. She was not crying, but she was persistent and unrelenting, and her anguish was visible. She kept saying to Dave and me, "Look, everything is going to be okay. You are assuming I am going to be in the hospital and not be able to move, but I will be fine."

She continued, "Mom, I am going to be home or . . . possibly in the hospital, true, but bored and with nothing to do. Please, this will give me something to do . . . Please." And she suggested she would make all the phone calls to remind people about the event and to invite those that were not responding. "Most of the work has been done. Mom, please don't cancel it because of me, please."

I was adamant that we did not need the extra stress and the uncertainty of it all, but Dave and Davey agreed with Christee. Raul's name needed to be honored. We had made the first steps toward our goal and there was no going back, according to Christee. And so it was settled; I would go ahead with the event.

I called the committee and informed them. Of course, they would see the event through on that day should I not to be present.

The event fell on Davey's birthday, August 25, 2006. We would celebrate his birthday too but privately among family and friends as we would all be there, already together.

When Christee went into the hospital at UCLA, we all panicked, but Christee just kept saying, "It's going to be okay. You'll see." She kept her cool and sense of humor, and that was good, but I was a nervous wreck!

I look back now, and I am so thankful that Christee had the good judgment not to allow me to cancel the event or the formal documents that were pending and needing completion to formalize the nonprofit status. She was right. Had I stopped it then, I would have never had the strength of mind to pick up the pieces and do it after all the events that followed.

Christee made calls to those that were invited and to her friends too, urging them to go, and even paid for a few of her friends to assist the event. She was concerned there were not that many reservations. Davey also called some of his friends and invited them to assist and celebrate the event and his birthday too. My kids were so supportive of the event and concerned that I would be disappointed if there was a low turnout that Davey also paid for some of his friends to go.

And on that August 25, 2006, with a sad and heavy heart and low spirit due to Christee's health, the Mayor Raul R. Perez Memorial Scholarship Fund was launched. I was full of resolve and, most importantly, with Raul in mind. The first event was held, and it was a success! I think I had even managed a smile to greet the guests. No one needed to know what was in my heart and mind other than the success of the event and that Raul's name would finally be honored in his city—the city that he loved so much.

It had been agreed that Christee would not go as the event was late in the afternoon and would carry on to the evening, and it was outdoors. I was concerned she would catch a cold or worse, pneumonia. She, of course, had argued, "I helped with it, so I should be there." But seeing that I was too stressed out, she had agreed not to go.

Was it Christee's love for life or was daring life itself her motivation to push and push the envelope to see where and how far she could go?

Christee showed up to the event hauling her oxygen tank and displaying a big smile. No pity and no sadness on her part. She was resolved to enjoy every minute of her life. She wanted to be around friends and family. "I couldn't miss the event and Davey's birthday too," she told me and hugged me, and in soft tone almost whispering said "Mom, everything looks nice."

My strength faltered and my heart ached, and I wanted to hold her and tell her how sick she was or maybe just run away and hide, not to face the truth. She was very sick; the illness was a matter of life and death, but her smile told me she needed to be there.

Not many of the friends and family knew what was going on, and now all of a sudden, they were asking what was wrong with Christee. Christee, with her smile, went around greeting people and easing their worries with "My doctor says it's asthma."

We all celebrated Raul's life and legacy.

True, all these years I felt God had not heard my prayers of healing for Raul, but on that day, I reflected. He may have indeed heard when I prayed that He take Raul when his pain had intensified and the end was near, and his despair and anguish for his wife and children were too much for him to bear, and I had prayed his suffering would end. "Let it be your will, Lord."

And seeing Christee that night, I hoped and I prayed that He would listen to my prayers of healing for Christee and that I would never have to ask Him to take her!

Chapter 54

The Emergency Room Trips

Late in the evening of August 28, 2006, Christee complained that her legs were hurting. She was crying from the pain. I had never seen her cry from pain. She cried if she was upset, angry, or wanted her way and didn't get it; but from pain, it was the first time. She had not cried or complained about her illness either since she had been diagnosed. I was so scared for my child.

I called Dr. Grossman at UCLA, and she spoke to Christee and, through the phone, provided a series of questions and items for us to check. Blood pressure was okay, and she had no fever. Her lower and upper extremities were not purple, and she had good color.

Dr. Grossman could not explain why she was experiencing so much pain and distress on her legs. Acetaminophen, she told us to give Christee for the pain with instructions to take her to the local hospital if she couldn't tolerate the pain and then to have the doctors transfer her to UCLA. She would give the transfer order.

In the middle of the night, we took her to the local hospital as the pain had intensified. They ran all her vitals, and by the time they finished, her pain had subsided; they sent her home.

The next day, she was fine. Her legs did not hurt, and she was in good spirits but was tired; she rested all day.

In the middle of the night again, on Wednesday, August 30, 2006, Christee woke up screaming. She was in such pain and was distraught. Her legs were hurting, and she kept saying they felt like they were burning, and she could not stand at all. She was cold but could not be covered as she could not bear the sheets or the blankets, although soft and light, to touch her skin.

We talked about taking her to UCLA. It was far, but the traffic would be lighter at that time of night. But her crying and labored breathing scared us, and we decided to take her again to the local hospital.

Dear God, even now that years have passed, I lay awake at night thinking what if we had made the drive to UCLA instead of taking her to the local hospital? I get up in the morning tired and realize how many scenarios I went through all night, yet the outcome is the same.

Christee's pressure was up, and her heart was in distress from the pain. I told them they needed to call UCLA, and they would give them the transfer order. Dr. Grossman was not answering my page but left various specific messages. They admitted her and immediately gave her pain medicines, and she went to sleep.

The next morning, Thursday, August 31, 2006, the admitting doctor ordered some exams. "Until Dr. Grossman calls and gives the order, we must treat her" were the doctor's instructions according to the nurses.

Dr. Grossman finally answered and said she had already requested the transfer, so we waited. I questioned the nurses throughout the day if they had the order, but they didn't know anything. I requested to see the elusive admitting doctor we had yet to see, but he was nowhere. "We paged him. He will be coming," the nurses would say, covering for his absence.

Christee was having trouble breathing, and the pain was coming back. She was running out of oxygen. It was the tank that we brought from home, and they were not doing anything. I requested to speak to the ombudsperson at the hospital, and the nurses said they would call them to come and see me, but I was done with waiting. I found out where they were and went up to their floor.

"The hospital does not have the insurance approval to send her on an ambulance yet." What? I was livid. Why hadn't they spoken to me about it earlier? It was after 5:00 p.m. now and the insurance office was closed. How could the hospital personnel be so inept? I was angry, and I was now lashing out and demanding to see the admitting doctor and the head nurse. "Where is the oxygen for my daughter?" I demanded.

A different nurse came and went to see Christee, and she immediately ordered that Christee be taken to intensive care. They had oxygen there.

All I could think was that it was a nightmare, and I wanted to wake up, but there was no waking up! We had been to that hospital many times before and the quality of care had been different. Why was all this happening to Christee? Providence was certainly not on her side . . .

Where was He? Didn't He know that she needed Him there?

On Friday, September 1, 2006, I called the insurance early in the morning, and they said they had not received any requests from the hospital for any transfers. The blame game had started, and my Christee was the innocent victim.

By midmorning, I had obtained the approval of the insurance only after I had once again complained and demanded to see the paperwork from their business office and that their submission to the insurance be done in my presence. The truth of the matter was that they had not sent it. With what purpose or motive? Exams and insurance money, I concluded, but perhaps, I was giving them too much credit. It could have been straight-out stupidity and ineptness.

I didn't want Christee to see or hear my aggravation and worry, so I had left the room to make the needed phone calls. Dave was there. Someone was always with her. I did not trust anyone in the hospital anymore.

Armed with the approval from the insurance, I called UCLA to confirm the transfer only to find out there was no longer a bed available for her. We would have to wait.

Dear Lord, it was definitely a nightmare, and it kept getting worse and worse by the minute.

Where was Your mercy? I had put her in Your hands. It was all up to You, and You were deaf to her and my prayers!

I continued calling throughout the day the admitting department and Dr. Grossman at UCLA for bed availability, but as the evening arrived, they informed me that there would not be any beds available for "transfers" until Monday as they had to reserve beds for "emergencies" as it was the Labor weekend.

Oh my God, I suddenly realized it was a long holiday weekend . . . Jesus, no, please. My Christee in a hospital on a holiday weekend!

I composed myself and went back to the intensive care unit and requested once again to speak to the doctor in charge.

Dr. Sarkeyr or Sarkerey—at this point I could care less if I have spelled his name correctly or not—he certainly did not deserve my respect then or ever. The nurse replied that the "doctor was expected" and would come to see me." Christee had been there three nights and two days, and he had not once gone to see her.

They tried to say he went to see her, but she was asleep, and it was a lie. I had been there day and night, and if I went home to shower and change, Dave, Ramon, or Davey would stay. She was never left alone. I questioned their ethics and Hippocratic Oath or their lack of them.

Late in the evening, he showed up to the unit. No one needed to tell me it was him. I knew all the faces by then, and his was the only unfamiliar one. I walked out of Christee's room and approached him, and his reaction was, "It was all a misunderstanding."

"A misunderstanding to what?" I said.

"You ordered exams that were not needed. You ignored Dr. Grossman's instructions to Christee's detriment." And I proceeded to list all the items I felt he had been negligent and derelict on as the admitting physician.

He was such a pathetic man. He offered no remorse for his omission of care or lack of regard for a patient and only felt more comfortable when the security guard came to stand next to him. Not once, was I rude or violent toward him, but I merely provided him with a litany of truths in advocating for my child.

However, my regret was not for his uncomfortable position or inadequacy, but in my haste to set him straight, I had not realized that Christee's room was too close, and the door had been left open; she had heard my discussion with him and now knew there was no bed and no transfer to UCLA until Monday, and now, she was also aware of my evident fear for her safety and health. The gravity of her state had been discussed although it was not eminent at the moment.

Chapter 55

Labor Weekend 2006

I walked back into the room, and Christee greeted me with a smile. Ramon had managed to fix the oxygen mask for her. The adult mask was too big for her small face, and the ties of the small one were not long enough. After all, it was for a child.

"Mom . . . am I really that sick?"

"No, Christee. You know me. I had to exaggerate so that he would listen and pay attention," I replied, managing a half smile.

The last thing I wanted was to lie to my child, but I could not tolerate to give her and Ramon any more grief or sorrow. He was standing there next to her, and they looked so happy and content about fixing the oxygen mask. I just smiled and told her how cute she looked with it and asked Dave to take a picture.

A nurse came and told us we all had to leave. I told her I would be staying the night. She dared tell me that Christee spoke English and was mobile, and there was no need for me to stay. I informed her to send the doctor in if she had a problem, but the head nurse heard and came to apologize and even offered to bring me a comfortable chair for my stay.

I was so confused. What had happened to this hospital? The turmoil, rudeness, and plain disregard for civility and kindness to patients and family were so prevalent and certainly not traits of a hospital. Why did I have to take her there? I still ask myself that over and over.

I kept track of Christee's vitals, type of medication, and the times they were administering them. I could provide Dr. Grossman with the information if needed.

On Saturday morning, September 2, they gave Christee pain medicine throughout the night as the pain on her legs had come back. I had told the doctor to see if he would order a CAT scan for the legs, and he said he would try to talk to Dr. Grossman. I did not believe him, so I kept paging her, but she was on holiday.

Christee woke up and was in good spirits, like always, and was hungry. It was early in the morning, and the change of nurses needed to be done. Breakfast would be after the new team took over.

The new team members were all nice and pleasant. The head nurse came and introduced herself to me and offered her unconditional services. They had most likely been warned. I no longer believed their lies, or perhaps, she really meant it and was genuinely concerned. Distrust—that is the problem when someone lies to you. You no longer trust anyone.

But as the day went on, I gave them all the benefit of the doubt and was pleasant again without judging them but still taking notes of medicines and times.

By midmorning, when it was time for her pain medicine, she asked that it not be given to her. She did not want to be sleeping if friends or family came to see her. The nurse and I told her that she should have it to avoid the pain from coming back, and she asked if the dose could be reduced. She wanted to be alert. The nurse checked the orders and agreed.

Throughout the day, she had company. She was pain-free and was breathing well. There was color to her cheeks, and her beautiful smile greeting the visitors convinced them that she was fine.

Sunday, September 3

There had been issues regarding the room she was in, and early in the morning, they had told us they would be moving her to a larger room.

The nurses had allowed her to wear her own pajamas and not to have the hospital gown during visits. Their attitude had changed tremendously since she had been brought down to the intensive care unit. One nurse had approached me and told me to move her out of there as soon as possible, saying, "This is not the right hospital for her." I told her the plan had been for her to be transferred to UCLA when she was first admitted, but they had failed to do the paperwork. "I am not surprised about it," she commented, gave me her name, and walked away.

Christee was thirsty, and all she wanted was the flavor waters. She had run out; Dave and I went to get more water. Davey and Ramon stayed with her and other friends who had come to see her.

She was in very good spirits and was pain-free, and again, she requested that the full dose of pain medicine not be administered, and I noted it when I came back.

Some family and friends showed up. Others sent word they would go the next day, and others expressed their regret for not coming. They "would rather not see her sick and at the hospital."

Christee was cheerful so many friends that cared and loved her had come to see her. Her smile was wide and visible, and the twinkle in her eyes was even more pronounced.

As I think back on that day, that moment, I can only say maybe, just maybe, if I had taken her home or driven her to UCLA myself . . . perhaps things would be different. I have all my notes of her vitals of that day, times and medicines that were administered, but I cannot look at them now. Was she well enough then? Could I have taken her out? It pains me so much to think that maybe she was doing well on that day, and I did nothing.

That evening, while we were all there—Dave, Davey, Ramon and I—Christee began to giggle and then the giggle grew into a snickering laugh. The laughter that began small was now a loud laughter. It was like she had just heard a joke that just lingered and then it was suddenly understood. It was a naughty laughter!

I remember asking her what was so funny, and she replied, "I just saw Tata. He was being wheeled across my door, and he turned to look at me, right next to where you are standing, Mom." Tata was her grandfather who had passed away two years earlier. She said, "I know it can't be. It's probably all the pain medicine that is giving me hallucinations."

We all laughed along with her, but in my heart, I knew that she had not taken much pain medicine throughout the day, and she had been alert all day. I didn't know what to think of it then, but now . . . I see the whole incident from a different perspective!

On Sunday night, everyone left, and Christee and I stayed, and we talked. She expressed how grateful she was to have so many people in her life that cared for her. "Mom, I am going to be okay, huh, Mom? We are going to beat this thing, right, Mom?"

"Yes, Christee. *Diosito* is going to heal you." I wanted to cry. I was distraught, and I was tired, but I needed to be strong like she was. I kissed her good night, and I read a magazine while she fell asleep.

Throughout the night, she kept waking up and taking the oxygen mask off. It was bothering her, and she was having trouble breathing. I called the nurses several times, and they came and adjusted the oxygen, and I questioned it. How did they know how much oxygen she could handle? And they would check her vitals and wait and adjusted until her breathing stabilized. It was a very restless night!

On Monday, September 4, Labor Day, I heard noise, and I woke up. Christee was getting out of bed. I jumped up and asked if she was all right. She apologized for waking me up; she needed to go to the bathroom. I reminded her that she was not allowed to get off the bed by herself and she laughed. "Mom, you look like caca. You need to rest." I ignored her comment and went to assist her. It was barely 5:00 a.m.

She lay down again but said she was not sleepy at all. "I had a good night's rest," she said. I knew she hadn't, but I didn't say anything. I tried to put my head back on her bed, leaning the chair closer to the bed, and she reached my head, stroked it, and reminded me I needed a haircut.

"Mom, go home and rest. You look very tired."

"I will, Christee, as soon as Dad comes over." Seeing that she wanted to talk and was not going to let me go back to sleep, I sat up straight on the chair and looked at her. She had good color on her face.

She insisted, "Mom, go home and rest, please. Today is going to be a very long and hard day. You should rest." I was tired, and it took me a few seconds to answer her. She repeated, "Go home, Mom, and rest."

"Why is it going to be a long and hard day today, Christee?"

"Oh, I don't know why," she said. "I want you to go to the store and buy something for me. I want you to wash my hair and put some ribbons on my hair. Bring the flower I like to wear on my hair. Mom, I want you to go home and rest and then come back. It's going to be a long day today. Make me look real pretty! There is going to be a lot of people here to see me."

I was not sleepy anymore. The light was on, and I could see the glow of happiness about her, and her voice was excited just talking about the people who were coming to see her. I said, "No, I'll go home when Dad comes over."

A nurse came in and alerted us of the shift change. I needed to get out of the room. I hadn't realized the time. We had been talking for a while.

All the nurses started to come into the room, and Christee looked at me with bright happy eyes and said, "Go home, Mom. Go home and rest. It is going to be a very long and hard day today. Bye, bye, Mom." She motioned with her tiny hand, and with a beautiful smile on her face, she said good-bye as I reluctantly left her hospital room.

With all the commotion and nurses in between us, and also telling me to step out, I walked out of the room without a kiss, without a hug, and without saying I love you and will be back soon.

What on earth was going on with me? In a daze, I got in the car and went home. I knew I had to hurry back. I just didn't know it would be that fast.

The drive was but a few minutes, and when I got home, Dave was in bed still. It was early, and he was not due in the hospital until after 8:00 a.m., but I was there, and I woke him up and hurried him to go to the hospital. I didn't want her alone, and he quickly got up and left. I was exhausted, but instead of getting in the shower, I decided to just lie down on top of the covers and fully dressed.

I had just closed my eyes when the phone rang and Dave said, "Get over here right away. Tell Ramon and Davey to get here now!" I jumped out of the bed and asked what was wrong, and he said, "Just get here now. She is not breathing!"

I hardly remember calling Davey and Ramon. I was on my way to the hospital and praying that I had heard David wrong.

I ran through the parking lot and into the hospital, and my heart was pounding. I had just left the hospital not even half an hour before. What had gone wrong? She was smiling when I left her . . . Oh, dear God, why did I have to leave? Why did she push me to leave? Why didn't she want me there? So many questions, but the truth was I should have never left.

I walked into the intensive care unit. I couldn't believe what I was seeing: a team of doctors in the room with her and David standing there next to them. They had just intubated her, and she was now slowly breathing with the assistance of a machine. Her fragile body laid there motionless and unconscious. I walked up to her and covered her. I didn't want her to be cold.

I turned to Dave and asked, "What happened?" He responded that when he walked into the room, she was breathing hard, and he had called the nurses, and they came, but Christee had looked at him and said softly, "Dad, I can't breath," and had gone into cardiac arrest.

What did the nurses do to her while I was gone? How much medication was she given? Did they change the pressure of the oxygen? I didn't realize I was thinking aloud. The doctor who was there next to her, reading the chart, was answering my question, but it didn't really matter what he said. I was not listening to anything. All I knew was my baby girl was not conscious or breathing on her own anymore.

I had prayed so much, and she had trusted God so much. We had both prayed He would cure her, and now . . . there was no smile on her face. *Why was He not answering her prayers?*

A Catholic with Catholic beliefs, I was angry. I didn't know what to do anymore. My heart said pray and He will listen, but I knew I had been praying and I had not heard or seen His responses. I didn't want to lose faith . . .

There was one more thing I needed to do. I had to prepare Christee for whatever it was that God may choose to do, and from the strength that I had seen in Christee before, I pulled myself together and I called a friend to ask that she arrange for the priest to come and see Christee.

Christee needed another sacrament. She had been baptized, had done her reconciliation, First Communion, and been confirmed as a Catholic, and now, the anointing of the sick. My heart pounded. I didn't want my denial upsetting anything, and I had to think of what was next. Oh Lord . . . the last rites! But she was unconscious now.

Labor weekend—the dreaded holiday weekends like when I lost my grandma, my mother, my father-in-law, and now . . . *I prayed that Christee would be spared, and He would listen.*

I tried hard to redirect my thoughts. I didn't want to think about what God had taken away before. The priest was only coming to bless Christee who would get better soon . . . *Yes, Christee would get better soon! Anointing of the sick was needed,* I thought.

God would not abandon Christee, not her. She had not once, since she had been diagnosed, been angry at Him. She had not cried out in despair. Instead she had prayed with faith and had silently resigned to His mercy and hoped for His will to cure her. Not once had she questioned God's will of her carrying the burden of these illnesses. I was sure He would not abandon her.

My thoughts and prayers were interrupted; Christee was having a second cardiac arrest, and Dave and I had to move away for them to work on her. It was like the night I had been at St. Francis when they were working desperately at resuscitating Mom.

A few minutes went by, and Christee was back, breathing!

The priest got there, and I think he anointed her with the holy oils. The truth is that I really don't know what happened next. It was like a dream where you see faces and hear voices, but you don't understand what is going on, who is there—nothing made sense.

I had lost sense of time. It appeared that an eternity had gone by. Then again, perhaps just a matter of minutes had gone by. I was totally lost.

I asked the doctor what was going on, and he kept saying he couldn't explain what was going on. He had been the doctor that had done some of the exams when she came in, and her heart and lungs had been strong enough. "This shouldn't be happening." But it was happening: I was slowly losing my baby girl.

She was having trouble breathing even with the machine. Another cardiac arrest, again defibrillation, more CPR. Her lifeless body was being battered, and it hurt me to see what was going on, but I understood they were working hard to resuscitate her to bring her back to life! After a few minutes, all over again and again. It was taking longer to bring her back, and the time she stayed with us, or her breathing, was shorter and shorter despite her being on the ventilator.

I don't know how long it was, but they kept trying to bring her back, and she was no longer reacting to anything they were doing. The doctor looked to Dave and me and said, "I am sorry, but she is no longer responding. She is gone."

It was like before: Dave, Christee, and I in a hospital. Just like when she was born when I hadn't heard her cry and had asked what was going on, but this time I knew!

She was no longer breathing, and they still kept giving her CPR, working on her. I could feel the compressions on her little chest, and my heart ached to think they were hurting her chest, and she was not reacting anymore, not even to the "shock paddles." Dave and I looked at each other. Out of nowhere, I began to speak to Christee and told her in a soft voice for her to hear me, "Christee, hold on to Jesus' hand. He is with you, and He will guide you home. Hold on to His hand." And Dave and I looked at her and told the doctors, "STOP."

I instantly knew I would never see her smile or hear her song again. She would never say, "Mom, Dad, I love you." Christee was pronounced dead at 4:00 p.m. on Monday, September 4. Undeniably, it had been a "long and hard day" as she had told me it would. I didn't get to wash her hair or put a ribbon on it. She was gone!

Her body was battered and bruised, and it still had to undergo more stress. The doctor suggested an autopsy to find out what went wrong and the cause of death. He was the pulmonologist, and he insisted her lungs had been strong enough earlier and couldn't believe why the cardiac arrest occurred.

Dave and I looked at each other, still in shock and with the piercing pain in our hearts. We had to gather our thoughts and decide. We also knew that Christee would have wanted an autopsy too and for Dr. Grossman to get the records.

The doctor would be able to study them and help someone else. Christee had asked that question of Dr. Grossman on that now distant day in August when she first met the doctor. "From whatever you find out about me or this illness in me, you will be able to help others?" The doctor had replied yes, and Christee had agreed to the treatment including chemotherapy if needed.

And we knew the answer had to be yes. It hurt us both to make such decision—the thought of her body being hurt even more—but it needed to be done in the hope that whatever they found could help someone else in the long run.

Chapter 56

More Promises

Christee certainly hadn't gotten a "break," not at all. Everything that could have gone wrong went wrong—the hospital, the simple transfer—and it was found out she had developed pneumonia, and no one noticed it, not even me. I had been vigilant to medicines, its administration, and times yet had not detected the development of pneumonia. In an instant, the breath from her body and spirit was gone forever.

The days that followed were as if I was in a fog-filled theater. There was so many people, so many questions, yet I couldn't see anyone clearly.

There was so much to do and no will to do any of it.

I don't remember when—that night, the next morning, or that afternoon—time just fused together at one point. Dave and I were holding each other and trying to collect our thoughts to be able to make the decisions on steps necessary for a burial. I reminded David of that one afternoon when we had gathered Christee and Davey in the kitchen and told them about our funeral arrangements having been made and where all our documents were kept.

Christee, being curious, asked "what type of arrangements does one make? Give me details."

We had told the children not to worry about plots for us or them as they had been purchased and paid for since 1986. Funeral arrangements, including flowers, were now purchased for Dave and me; they would not have to worry about anything. Davey hadn't said much, but Christee wanted to see the file I had on my hand to see the type of casket and type of flowers I had ordered.

I remember telling her that wasn't important. What was important was for them to know that everything was ready and paid for and where the paperwork was located and that all our wishes as to the service were made in the event that something happened to us.

Christee was still interested in looking, and I finally showed her the file, and she said, "I am going to change the flowers for you. I don't want roses." I replied that it was my funeral and my arrangements, and I wanted roses.

Christee then had stopped being funny and, with a serious tone of voice, had said, "Mom, if I happen to die first, before you, promise me my flowers will be the big pink stargazers. Promise me, Mom." I told her I didn't know which ones were the stargazers, and I would get her roses if they were cheaper. But she said, "I don't want roses. I want big pink stargazers. Mom, also buy me a real pretty dress. Don't put on me an old dress." We had laughed, and I had told her I would put on her a certain dress that I knew she disliked, and we laughed some more.

But she was suddenly serious and said, "Mom, I am not joking. I want an open casket. I want a flower on my hair, a pretty dress, and big pink stargazers."

"Okay, Christee," I replied, and Dave and Davey had laughed. Davey commented that he wouldn't mind being buried on the side of the house next to the bunny, turtle, and fish he had long ago buried.

I had promised her I would bury her in the manner in which she had indicated. Of course, I never would have thought I have to do it!

I told Dave I would like to send her off in a white wedding dress. She had been so enthusiastically looking at bridal magazines and had several picked out. He agreed with me. I went and shopped for one the next day.

Did she know? Did she feel it, or was she just being practical?

She had given directions to her funeral. How many of us, young or old, are so afraid to make those decisions, knowing that it is the only certainty in life: death!

Purchasing a bridal gown without a bride, "There are no exchanges. Are you sure she will like it, and will it fit?" were the questions and statements made to me at many of the bridal shops I visited. I didn't just want a white dress, but I was trying to find one of the gowns she had picked or, at least, one that resembled the ones she liked.

As painful as it was, Dave and I were able to fulfill my promise to Christee. She had an open casket celebration, and she looked beautiful in her white wedding dress, beautiful makeup with a small pink stargazer flower behind her ear, and the church was adorned with big pink stargazers. She was a beautiful bride.

Chapter 57

A Resting Place

What? I couldn't believe what I was seeing. Here we go again. Couldn't anything go right for Christee?

At the cemetery, the day before the funeral, I had insisted to go see the actual plots. I had not been there for so long. I couldn't remember where exactly they were located. I wanted to see them now. I didn't want to wait for the next day.

The gentleman assisting us took us to the place immediately. We had bought the plots back in '80s, and it was one of the original areas of Rose Hills Park, overlooking the city and close to my mother's plot.

When we arrived to the place, we found out there was a water pipe broken, and the whole area was flooded. No one had seen it or reported it yet. It was a total disaster; there was no way a funeral could be held there.

The park maintenance people kept saying they would fix it in time for the funeral and "It should be dry by tomorrow." We disagreed and immediately requested relocation, but they kept insisting it would all be okay. "Do you want a slip and fall accident and a lawsuit over this?" They had a change of heart and agreed to a transfer. I was upset about the whole thing. All those years knowing our final resting place would be next to my parents' family plot, and now, it had to change. But of course, I also needed a proper and suitable place to give Christee a burial, and the guests' safety had to be considered too. A new place needed to be selected. So much grief and heartache and still one more decision to be made. After they showed us several places available, we made a choice.

When we were told a little more about the place selected, we accepted with joy and silently understood and believed there was a higher reason why Christee had been relocated. The new plots were located farther up the mountain where the undeveloped area abuts the manicured fields, where they are abundant with bunnies, reindeer, coyotes, and other special creatures that Christee would have definitely enjoyed. She would have requested the change herself had she known!

Perhaps, in my grief-stricken mind, I imagined that she would be tending to the animals or having her pets, and that made me happy. I didn't care if anyone thought I was going nuts. There was at least something that I could smile about.

The vigil was beautiful. There was so many people there gathered to see her off and elevate their prayers to God on her behalf. There was music and songs. I am sure she would have picked those songs herself and sang along, or perhaps she did sing along.

And moving through the motions, I prayed. I prayed for Christee's soul and for strength.

I was sad; my heart was broken, and my head felt empty, like in a deep sleep, wanting to wake up but lucid enough in my thoughts. I told my husband, "Do not let me cry in the funeral. Do not let my anguish disrespect Christee's memory and celebration. It is about Christee's life and remembrance. It is not about me or anyone else but her. Let us be strong. As strong as she was."

The next day, at the grave site, only one song was played, and it was the last song she had composed and recorded with Ramon's assistance, and now, she sang for all those present.

The One for Me
Christee Lee Rivera

I have been broken, and I have been lost
Well, I, I was defeated, and I, I was crossed
Tell me now, are you the one for me
Tell me now, are you the one I see in my dreams
You, you stand before me and say you love me
And you, you can't wait to search my soul oh
Tell me now, are you the one for me
Tell me now, are you the one I see in my dreams
Cause I don't want to cry
And please, oh please don't lie
[Musical interlude]
Why does love hurt so much oh ooh
And why did it take so damn long to find you
Tell me now, are you the one for me
Tell me now, are you the one for me
I have been broken, and I, I've been lost
You came and flew me away

As the sound of the melody was heard and the words followed with the beautiful message, a gust of wind swiftly rushed through the trees, and the chimes on the trees had a heavenly tone to them. Her presence was felt by me and everyone there as some commented. Her send-off was definitely spiritual in nature. Even now when I hear her song, I question if it had been composed for Ramon or, in fact, for God himself. Would you like to hear her song?

But my strength faltered as the casket, now in the vault, was being slowly lowered. This was no longer a dream, no longer an expectation to wake up, no longer the hope of His miracle that she would be cured and live. And as the dirt began to fall on the casket, I could no longer bear the pain. I was a coward, and I wanted to run, to hide, and to leave that place. Slowly, not to upset anyone, I walked to my car and got in and said, "Good-bye, my love."

Chapter 58

Sympathy

So many people, so much commotion, so many telephone calls and cards, and so much food. Then, all at once, silence and then everyone was gone.

The next few months were as if I was on automatic pilot. I got up, showered, and went to work, and when the afternoon came, I went home. On and on, the days and weeks went on. There were so many days, weeks, and months that I went to work, and not once did I pick up the phone or even turn the lights on in the office. It was all a charade; there was no work for me to do. I wasn't taking any new work, but I couldn't stay home and give Dave more to worry about.

"Don't cry. Be happy. You are not letting her rest," friends would say, and they meant well, but it did me no good. Instead, it put me in despair. *What kind of God would allow that? I questioned.*

"She is better off now. She is not here, suffering,"

"Really? Then why were *they* still here if dead was best?" I retorted. And slowly, anger and resentment were building. I didn't want to hear those well-intentioned people tell me, "I know exactly what you are going through. My niece died too." How dare they!

Why couldn't they just hug and kiss and make me feel warm and cared for like Marika and Dale did? They sent cards every week with no expectations of a response but just reached out and let me know they cared, and their prayers for Christee, Davey, Dave, and me were there.

The first Thanksgiving and Christmas came and went, and the anger kept building up.

My family and friends avoided mentioning Christee's name as if she had only been a figment of my imagination and had not existed. The resentment toward them was getting worse.

I can see now there was fear and hesitation on their part to mention her and to avoid "bringing me memories and pain." But in their caution, they were hurting me more. Didn't they care? Didn't they miss her? And didn't they want to share their memories of her with me? Why not ask the person how they feel about it instead of assuming?

The winter came; Davey didn't want to see me cry and would get very upset and snap at me for crying. Davey was distant and had conditioned and put up a shield around himself from any pain, almost disconnected from everyone. And Dave, he was quiet and somber. He and I had only cried once together. He was being tough and strong for me, but Davey was right. "Dad lost his daughter too. You are not the only one grieving." And poor Ramon was grieving on his own. I didn't know how to help him and encourage him to seek out professional help. I was worried about everyone but felt so useless and inadequate. All I wanted was to be left alone.

The family was drifting apart. There was no laughter, music or song, or even the smell of freshly baked cookies anymore.

I knew I was spiraling down but wanted to keep up with work ethic, commitments, and appearances, and I went here and there like everything was "normal."

Eight months had passed since my Christee was gone. I was being in automatic mode: sleeping only if I took sleeping pills, eating only if I forced myself to. On this day, I found myself sitting in church. It was Good Friday 2007.

Just sitting there, looking around like if it was my first time in church, seeing the people gather for services. The church was rapidly filling up, yet I felt so lonely, an emptiness I thought I never felt before and a sorrow beyond comprehension, and I began to quietly cry the type of tears that only come with despair. I had felt the same way when Christee died, on that distant day of September 4, 2006, yet so visibly present like it was just the day before.

I was trying to suppress my weeping. Suddenly, I couldn't breathe! I looked up to ask for help, and I saw the Jesus on the cross—the Christ, the all-loving and merciful father—and out of nowhere, I felt anger, betrayed by someone whom I loved and in whom I had placed my trust and had dedicated my children to . . . and *where was He when Christee and I prayed for His love and mercy? He had remained silent to our supplications.*

I looked around, still feeling a shortness of breath, and all I could think was *What am I doing here? What a hypocrite! I am angry. Angry at you. You took my baby, her laughter, her dreams, her songs.*

To my surprise, as if I had been commanded to get up, I got up and took a small step out of the pew and then another step, and I felt my stride was gaining speed, and my step was fast and steady. I knew what I was doing. I was walking away from someone that had not heard Christee's prayers and took her without regard of her dreams and plans, where He was included too.

There was no reason for me to be there, none at all, and the anger grew as I made my exit, promising never to come back.

Chapter 59

Reflections

Almost one year had gone by since the day I walked out of the church, angry with a longtime friend that had not been there for my Christee and feeling I didn't need or want that friendship, but I was not happy with that severed relationship either.

In my heart, I still had faith, but it was the anger that had driven me away.

I had begun to write about Christee and Christee's life early on when I visited the cemetery. I didn't just want to cry and dwell on those ill-fated days but wanted to hold on to Christee: who she was, her happiness, all those memories we had built together as a family, and all those lives she had touched, mine included. They brought more joy than to continue rehashing the sad and dark days of her death.

As I kept writing I realized I had been a witness, not just to the miracle of life itself, but to many other instances where God had been alongside Christee's life. He had not forsaken her.

When Christee was born, she was not breathing, yet He gave her the breath of life for twenty-three years when He could have taken her then.

And what about when she fell in the pool or crashed the car or when in despair due to her lupus diagnosis had ran away and had slept on that park bench?

I often told the children the stories of their births. I always omitted from the story the part that Christee was not breathing when she was first born.

The children loved to sit with me looking at their newborn pictures, and I loved remembering those beautiful and happy moments. They would be amazed and mesmerized as to how tiny they were and how Christee had a smile at all times. Now I wonder, *Did she know?*

Cystic fibrosis, asthma, and scleroderma—all lung diseases.

My heart tightens; my voice crackles and tears come to my eyes, but I don't want to cry. I don't want to remember that now—not now and not anymore.

And little by little, there was no more anger, and I realized I needed to make peace with my friend. He had in fact been there for her and had heard her prayers on July 31, 2006, when she had been diagnosed with scleroderma.

It was the only time her voice and heart had expressed hopelessness and desolation when the doctor told her about having scleroderma. "No, not that, God." She had known what scleroderma was all about.

I had wrongly accused my friend of not being there for her! *He had indeed heard her prayers. He had spared her of the awful pain and had not allowed her to lose her love for life, her laughter, and her free spirit.*

I needed to thank Him for all those days, weeks, months, that He had allowed me to be Christee's mom!

I didn't recognize the magnitude of the events as they had unfolded, from birth to death. And I reflected on how blessed I had been. She had lived! I had held her. He had chosen ME to be Christee's mom, and even if it had only been a day or twenty-three years, as it was in Christee's case, I would forever be grateful.

Dear Lord, thank You for opening my heart and eyes.

Chapter 60

Her Embrace and Her Ring

I needed to go to church and thank Him, ask for forgiveness and make peace!

There was so much going on with the three of us. All in the hopes to keep busy, ignore the evident, and allow time to pass. I was in the middle of moving out of the South Gate office. All my savings were gone.

I needed work but still could not move forward to go get the contracts I had once given up because I didn't feel competent during my grieving time to perform to the best of my abilities. I was in the middle of moving out of the South Gate office; all savings were gone. A small office with fewer expenses would do until I could regroup and decide what to do.

Davey had moved out of the house in anger because I had not yet stopped crying from the loss of Christee, and now, I was lonelier than ever and crying even more. I missed Davey.

Dave had gone to Arizona each and every weekend since he bought the "Christee House," a river house, back in April 2007. "Because Christee and I were in the middle of looking to buy a house" had been his reasoning. She was gone, yet he bought a house she never saw or would ever see. It hadn't made any sense then or now, but he bought it anyway. Without a doubt, we all grieve differently!

March 15, 2008 was another day without Christee. Dave left for Arizona, angry at me for not going with him. In his anger, and still grieving, he managed to still be kind and courteous and take my father along with him to keep him company, and I appreciated that very much.

But on this day, two things were on my mind: one, to clean Christee's workstation at my office without crying or reliving the painful memories, and two, to go to church and pay my respects to Ricardo's parents who had invited me to Ricardo's memorial Mass. But how could I accomplish going to Mass if I had not yet made peace with my God and had vowed never to go back? *Would He forgive me?* I wondered. Perhaps today was a good day to go and make peace with my friend.

It was getting late, and I had procrastinated long enough, and I began to empty the drawers, but I had to read the notes—what if they were important? And they were . . .

They were Christee's notes and read like this:

> *Came in at 10:00 a.m., was hungry.*
> *Went to breakfast 10:30.*
> *Lunch at 12:00 p.m. to 1:15 (I went to pick up the food;*
> *Mom paid for it). I finished my homework.*
> *Left at 4:00 p.m., Mom owes me six hours.*

And another note read,

> *Prepare a contract to pay Mom for cell phone.*
> *Davey and I will sign. I have to make sure I pay.*
> *I know Mom; she will cancel it otherwise.*

There were many notes, and I did no cry but savored the moment. *We would have all laughed if we could have read these notes years later all together.*

I finished cleaning her station, and I had not cried nor was I angry. I felt happy and I felt joy and I thought, *I am going to be all right.*

I suddenly realized the time. I had promised Ofie I would come home and take care of Yoly and Ramoncito. She needed to run an errand, and I rushed out of the office. I felt that my step was lighter, and there was a renewed energy in my body, and I even thought there was a smile on my face.

I navigated through the street traffic and got on the 105 Freeway. I definitely had a smile on my face then. I was thinking of Christee's notes and the times that we had spent together at that office, talking, arguing, and just working silently.

The traffic was light to medium for a Saturday afternoon and I began to move lanes. My exit would be on my left-hand side. I looked in my rearview mirror and then to my left and up in front, and there it was! The most amazing thing was happening to me.

You must pause and think before you go any further in the story.

Do you have faith? Do you believe in God and His miracles?

Because I do! And I had thought I had witnessed them all but not yet. He still had one more for me to witness and share with you!

I was looking at the horizon toward my upcoming exit, the carpool lane traffic on my left and plenty of cars in front of me, and then, for an instant, there was nothing: no cars, no traffic but only my Christee's face! She was not in the car with me. She was not on the windshield but farther ahead in front of me!

Yes, like a dream, I saw Christee's face with her beautiful smile and the sparkle in her eyes. She was extending her arms out to me, like in a greeting, and then I felt her warm embrace—the one which I longed for and had prayed for so much. The one embrace I had wished I had given her that day when I left the hospital.

She didn't say anything to me, but her face was radiant and happy, and that beautiful smile that I had missed so much was there right in front of me!

And then, in an instant, it was gone!

Oh my God, I thought, *what just happened?* And I immediately looked to my right and to my left and saw cars and cars in all lanes. I was driving. I was still on the 105!

I saw cars passing me, and I saw my exit and took it, and I knew I was awake, but I was anxious and nervous. I couldn't explain what had just happened.

My initial thought was, *Oh my God, I am going crazy.* Yet I still had that warm feeling in my body, just like when someone hugs you and holds you for a while, and a happy and peaceful feeling was in me. There was so much joy that I began to cry, but this time, the tears were of happiness and joy.

I was out of the freeway now and on the street, and I went into the parking lot of the CVS on Imperial and Studebaker. I was fully awake, and I had not dreamed or hallucinated. I had seen Christee's face and her beautiful smile, and she had hugged me. I was alone; no one else had seen her. But I knew it was real, I could still feel the warm sensation on my body of someone having touched me, embraced me.

I needed to call Dave and let him know what had just happened. I needed validation that I was awake, not crazy, and that my prayers of seeing her one more time had been answered!

I felt like God had forgiven me already and was asking me to seize my faith and believe in Him again, and YES, I believe!

David did not answer his cell phone, and I kept redialing. I needed to tell someone, yes, to confirm that I was awake, that I was coherent, and that I was not dreaming, but he was not answering the phone, and I left several messages.

I was still at the parking, not wanting to leave, yet I knew Ofie was waiting for me. But I was afraid of leaving the parking lot, of time passing by, and forgetting what had just happened.

I took a paper from the glove compartment, but I didn't have a pen in my purse, and I was frustrated and then I thought of calling a friend, and I did. I called Gigi, a sweet young lady who had also lost her mother and knew about the sadness, grief, and pain of losing a loved one. She had been a source of comfort to me on the early days after Christee had died. I thought of the time when she told me, "You are not ready yet. When you are ready, you will feel or see Christee next to you." I didn't know what to think of what she was telling me then.

Gigi was not answering either, and I left a message too, a simple and brief message, just for her and *me* to know what just happened. No details at all. She later told me that, from my voice, she knew what had happened to me on that afternoon.

I finally left the parking lot and made it to Ofie, who was waiting for me on the driveway.

That evening, I was full of happiness and excitement. I felt that I needed to go to Ricardo's memorial Mass. I needed to be at church, and more than ever, I needed to thank God and to ask Him for forgiveness for being angry at Him and having abandoned the church.

I had such a joyful feeling in me, one that I had not had for a long, long time, since Christee had been diagnosed. I kept calling David, but there was no answer.

Ricardo's Mass was held at St. Matthias church, which holds so many beautiful and sad memories for me. The Mass was beautiful, and I had enjoyed the celebration very much. I felt welcomed in church and by the Paz family. I remembered how happy I was when Christee and Ramon got engaged, to know Christee would be part of the Paz family whom I have always appreciated. I felt I was at the right place and among the right people. I felt loved. *She is now in heaven with Ricardo, my best friend. She is indeed part of God's family and the Paz family too,* I thought.

I called David again before I went to bed, and I was annoyed that I could not reach him to share my wonderful experience.

Even after a few hours had passed, I still felt the joy but began to feel apprehension that my mind was playing tricks on me, and I did not know what David would say or how he would react to my account of the experience I had.

Oh Dave, guess what happened today? "I saw Christee's face with that same beautiful smile as she always had, and she was right there in front of me and slightly reaching down to me. She extended her arms and hugged me, and I felt the warmth of her arms around me and her face next to mine." What would he say? . . . And I fell asleep.

Chapter 61

Palm Sunday

The phone woke me up and it was Dave, and his voice was full of excitement and I wanted to tell him what happened to me, but he just kept saying, *"Guess what happened to me yesterday? Guess what I found yesterday? You won't believe what I found?"* I held my excitement and said to him, "What happened? What did you find?"

"Christee's ring! I found Christee's ring!"

"What ring? What are you talking about?" I was confused, not understanding what he was talking about.

"Her high school class ring."

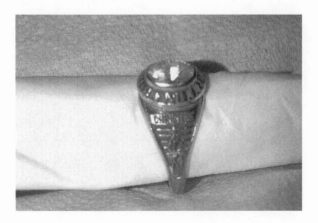

With exasperation I interrupted him. "No, David, you are mistaken. Christee lost her ring almost right after she graduated in 2001, and she was never at the river house. You didn't buy the house until April of 2007. You and Christee had gone house hunting, but you told me not at this house. So you are mistaken. It cannot be Christee's ring."

"I know all of that, but it is her ring. It has her name and the name of the school and the school mascot. It is her ring, and I found it outside our house, on the gravel patio next to the car keys, which I had dropped earlier. I know it sounds impossible, and I thought about it all night, but it is Christee's ring, and I found it! I have it, and I'll show it to you when I get back home."

I was listening to him, but as he was explaining, I noticed the excitement and happiness in his voice, and I began to think about my own experience, and I asked him, "Dave, when did this happen? When did you find the ring? Give me details!"

He was excited and happy to continue. "Yesterday afternoon. I had gone to the market, and when I was bringing in the groceries, I dropped the keys, but I couldn't pick them up and forgot all about them. Your dad reminded me about the keys when it began to rain, and I went outside, and they were there and, next to them, the ring, with all the gravel. If the keys had not been next to it, I would have never found it."

I knew right then and there that I was not crazy and that it had to be Christee's ring. That our faith was still with us, and this time, I had recognized the experience, the miracle, as it happened, and I thanked Him.

I told Dave that I had been calling him the day before in the afternoon to tell him what had happened to me, that I had hardly slept thinking about it, and that what he was telling me was a reaffirmation of our faith. God had not abandoned us. He had allowed him, Dave, and me to experience Christee's presence one more time and at the same time. Although he was in Arizona and I in California, Christee had been with both of us at the same time and, perhaps, asking that we not argue and fight but that we find harmony and happiness again.

We could hear each others' happiness, and we believed Christee had been with us the day before and now was smiling at us.

My theory was that, once again, as she had done before when she had heard us arguing, she would say, *"Hey, you two are acting like Tata and Granma. Cut it out."* We had been arguing; David had left for Arizona upset that I did not go with him, and I was not happy that he bought that house. I felt he bought the house for all the wrong reasons. He had promised to buy her a house, but Christee was not there, and we were arguing. *I think Christee wanted us to know she was there and not happy that we were arguing.*

I could hardly wait for Dave to get back. I wanted to see the ring. I knew it was Christee's, and I wanted to see it!

When Dave pulled the ring out of his pocket, *it was Christee's ring*, and I don't know why, but I immediately tried it on, and it fit! It fit! Christee's hands were so petite compared to mine. She could borrow all my jewelry but never my rings, and I was happy about that as she would lose them, I was sure, just like she lost many of my earrings.

I now wear her high school graduation ring that miraculously fits my not-so-petite hand's right ring finger. I wear it proudly as a reminder of that wonderful day during Holy Week when my faith was renewed. I can still see her face and feel her warm embrace when I close my eyes, and yes, I thank God every day for allowing me to live and to have my beautiful memories, including the sad ones.

I thank Him for the experience of having my children, the love of Christee and Davey, and having held her in my arms and calling her my child, *mi niña*, for those wonderful twenty-three years full of MIRACLES that now I am able to see, recognize, and treasure them all.

And I tell YOU, do not despair, do not torment yourself, and above all, do not be angry with our Father. Pray for a miracle. Have faith, and it too will happen and reveal itself to you. He does respond, perhaps not in the manner that we want, but we must believe first. He knows what is in our heart and what is best for us and our loved ones.

I now believe because of my faith that Christee's life had a purpose, one that was fulfilled.

Christee knew what scleroderma was when she was first diagnosed. It was the only time I saw her with anguish and despair. I now know what a terrible disease it is, full of pain, agony, and hopelessness, and I am happy that God did not allow the pain, despair, and agony to come to Christee. Instead, she left with her wonderful smile, saying, "Bye, Mom. Go home and rest." What a loving and unselfish child He had allowed me to have, care for, and yes, to learn from. We all have a purpose in life, and mine, perhaps, was to witness Christee's love of life and share her story with you.

My pain is still deep and very vivid and the emptiness in my heart is big, so big; yet the memory of holding her close to me and feeling her tiny hands on my face and later on her calling me mom is enough to quench my sadness and dry my tears; To live another day and share my story about her life.

Whatever your faith or believes are You are not alone in your pain. I am sure there are so many people around you that love you and care for you and miss your love one too. You have the right to be angry and upset if you want. And you have the right to cry as much as you want. You too have a purpose in life, and when you are ready you can reflect and treasure those memories, with and about your love ones, write them down find the miracles of life and share them with others, who like us have lost a love one and are lost themselves.

Find help if you need help and learn again to live, love and enjoy life and laugh at those memories you built with your love ones and bring joy to your heart.

Open your heart and see.

Epilogue

Only One Promise Remained

"Promise me you'll do something, Mom, so it won't happen to anyone else. He should have seen those results and told me about them."

"Yes, Christee, I promise you, but not right now."

"Thank you, Mom."

A lawsuit against her doctor, the admitting doctor, and the hospital was filed, not for monetary gain, but to compel that the policies and procedures of all those involved be reviewed and changed.

On December 2008, a settlement was reached with all parties and particular offices agreeing to change various polices and procedures including the following:

An admitting doctor must see their patient immediately upon admission and not by phone only.

Transfers to other hospitals, when the orders are in, must be immediately expedited, and the patient and family must be kept aware of the developments.

And as to Christee's primary doctor, he agreed that all lab results would not be put inside the files prior to his review, and office policy and procedures would be reviewed and changed. He also agreed to make a donation to the lupus foundation. I did not request the donation to be in Christee's name but to be made as a general donation for all those beautiful people with that disease.

There was no award for money requested or received.

I had promised Christee I would do something about it so what happened to her would never happen to anyone else. And on a cold December morning, I went to Christee's grave site, and there, with a sad heart, I read the agreements to her, letting her know that I had fulfilled all my promises to her.

Love, Mom

Yesterday, today, and tomorrow.

Did You Know?

According to the Eastern Orthodox Church as well as the Byzantine Catholic Church, the day before Palm Sunday is celebrated as *Lazarus Saturday*. This day, together with Palm Sunday, hold a unique position in the church year as days of joy and triumph between the penitence of Great Lent and the mourning of Holy Week (*Wikipedia*).

I did not know anything about the day before Palm Sunday or about "Lazarus Saturday." Because of the significance of the experience that both Dave and I had, on that day, I looked up the date and found out about this. I was very happy to find the meaning of that day, the day before Palm Sunday, and its meaning in the church.

Do you see what I see?

Only God could have sent Christee to us for one more day—one more time as it once again reiterated to me that it was indeed a *Godsent day to me*.

Meet My Family

Thank you,

To all our family and friends, a most sincere and heartfelt thanks for visiting Christee, bringing her flowers, candy, stuffed animals and dolls, and yes, a bridal magazine, while she was at the hospital. You all gave her joy, hope, and happiness. It will forever be appreciated and remembered.

And to Laura, my most appreciative thanks. Please know that I will forever be grateful for your love and unselfishness in offering to donate your lung to Christee as soon as you found out about her being on the donor list. She always held you in a very special place in her heart and so do I.

Thank you to all our family and friends who gave us love, heartfelt sympathy, and plenty of prayers at the time of our loss. We will forever be grateful and appreciative of all you did for us.

But I specially want to thank Marika. She was my friend of only a short time at the time I lost my Christee, yet she was with me every step of the way. When everyone was gone and all the sympathy cards stopped coming and the phone didn't ring anymore, Marika was there.

Marika had the right words time after time. When I felt hopeless, she brought me hope, and week after week and month after month, her cards arrived home. She wasn't asking for a response. She wasn't asking to be acknowledged. All she wanted was for Dave, Davey, and me to know that someone cared, and we felt her love and concern. And I began to eagerly wait, week after week, month after month, for her cards as they gave me hope and words of encouragement and kept reminding me of the conversation we once shared about faith. Thank you, my dear friend!

I also want to apologize to many of you who offered words of condolences for my rudeness. I wasn't ready to hear "She is better off now," "Don't cry because you won't let her rest in peace," or "I know what you are going through. I lost my niece too." My sensitive heart rejected your words, but I now know you meant well. Forgive my abrasiveness.

I love and appreciate all of you.

"Silence is a source of great strength."

—*Lao Tzu*

Index

Made in the USA
San Bernardino, CA
13 February 2013